# STRONGEST IN THE BROKEN PLACES

*PLACES*

A Story of Spiritual Recovery

# Dan Harrison

Edited by Maria Henderson

INTERVARSITY PRESS
DOWNERS GROVE, ILLINOIS 60515

*InterVarsity Press is the book-publishing division of InterVarsity Christian Fellowship, a student movement active on campus at hundreds of universities, colleges and schools of nursing in the United States of America, and a member movement of the International Fellowship of Evangelical Students. For information about local and regional activities, write Public Relations Dept., InterVarsity Christian Fellowship, 6400 Schroeder Rd., P.O. Box 7895, Madison, WI 53707-7895.*

*All Scripture quotations, unless otherwise indicated, are from the Holy Bible, New International Version. Copyright* © *1973, 1978, International Bible Society. Used by permission of Zondervan Bible Publishers.*

*Cover illustration: Roberta Polfus*

*ISBN 0-8308-1720-4*

*Printed in the United States of America* ∞

**Library of Congress Cataloging-in-Publication Data**

*Harrison, Dan, 1941-*
        *Strongest in the broken places: a story of spiritual recovery/*
    *by Dan Harrison; edited by Maria Henderson.*
            *p. cm.*
        *Includes bibliographical references.*
        *ISBN 0-8308-1720-4*
        *1. Harrison, Dan, 1941-          2. Christian biography.        I. Title.*
*BR1725.H2393A3      1990*
*209'.2—dc20                                                            90-45669*
*[B]                                                                        CIP*

13   12   11   10   9   8   7   6   5   4   3   2   1
99   98   97   96   95   94   93   92   91   90

# Preface

Writing this book involved facing once again my brokenness while reviewing experiences through which I felt much pain. Also, it caused me to analyze what has changed, is changing and why. In the process I recounted part of the record of God's faithfulness in the healing process, which is ongoing.

This book obviously represents my viewpoint on the stories and only I can be held responsible for their lack of accuracy.

At the same time, this book represents the role of others, too numerous to name, that have helped me both in the recovery process and others with the book itself.

I want to acknowledge my family and thank them.

Thanks goes to persons who read the manuscript and made helpful suggestions. Special appreciation goes to my editor Maria Henderson, without whose help the project might not have been finished. Thanks also to Don Stephenson for his encouragement and support in the project.

# Introduction:
# A Story of
# Hope & Healing

ugust 10, 1986. It was our twenty-fifth wedding anniversary, and our four daughters were taking us out for a special celebration. We ate at our favorite restaurant in the Chinatown section of Los Angeles, reminiscing and enjoying one another's company.

As we were finishing our meal, our second daughter, Melody, announced: "Mom and Dad, in anticipation of this significant event we did a lot of thinking about how we might honor you with a gift. We hope you like it, even though it is a bit unusual."

Paula, our eldest, continued: "You have been together for

twenty-five years, and we have been a part of most of those years. We have been together almost all of that time, and we are very close emotionally. As we look toward the next twenty-five years, we realize that we will be separating physically, but we don't want to become less close emotionally or less committed to one another."

We were all very aware that Paula was leaving in two days for a year of teaching English in China. Tonya would be heading back to college in Texas in a few weeks. Melody was attending college nearby, and even Holly, our youngest, was in junior high school. Our nest was emptying.

Then Melody pulled out two small ring boxes. The girls had bought a "family ring" for each of us. They had created quite a stir in the jewelry store when they asked for six wedding bands! The rings were to remind us of our commitment to one another, no matter where we might be.

While driving home, I remarked that our family was not the average, garden-variety American family. We had something very precious, which we all valued and wanted to preserve. The family rings symbolized our love for one another and our recognition that our family's closeness did not happen by accident.

It may be difficult for some people to imagine a family like ours. I would never have believed a story like that when I was the age of my daughters. I couldn't imagine a family where love was expressed openly and where respect and honest communication developed healthy, secure individuals who wanted to be with each other.

The family I grew up in was nothing like the family I am part of now. My parents loved us and each other, but in many ways their love was damaged by the dysfunctional dynamics of our family. I grew up in an environment where I was unsure of my father's love. I felt criticism and disapproval at every turn and became an insecure, rebellious youth. I didn't think I was worth much to anyone; I didn't believe that I had anything to contribute to society. For many years I was crippled by the experiences of my childhood.

But this isn't a story of defeat and despair; it's a story of hope and healing. Our family is not perfect, but my wife and I have managed to establish a healthy home life and raise four women whose strength of personality, character, talent and vision surprise even us. For more than twenty years we have served in mission agencies, fulfilling a variety of roles from teaching to administration. We have seen the impact of our lives and work in all kinds of ways, and the opportunities stretched out before us continue to excite and inspire us.

The road I've walked from the pain of my dysfunctional family to the joys of my life today has been characterized by struggles and false starts as much as by victories and smooth progress. I'm still on that road; there are still remnants in my life that I have to deal with, places where I'm trying to learn that lesson for the tenth or twentieth or hundredth time. I hope that some of the lessons I've learned and the way I've experienced Jesus' promise that "my grace is sufficient for you, for my power is made perfect in weakness" (2 Cor 12:9) will encourage others who struggle with the scars of a dysfunctional family experience. There is hope for broken people; that's the message of the good news.

# 1

## *How Can God Use Me?*

I n 1953, when I was twelve years old, my seventeen-year-old brother, Frank, was home from the Marine Corps. As youngest of the family, I idolized my older brothers, especially Frank.

Cherishing moments with him, I joined him in the two-holer outhouse. He was smoking a Camel cigarette, so I asked if I could smoke one. He answered, "Naw, you wouldn't like it. It'd make you sick. Besides, Dad would get mad as hell at me, just like he always does." I finally persuaded him to give me a cigarette. It was my first. It tasted terrible. I didn't really smoke it, just puffed on it.

Then I bumped into my Dad on the way into the house. "You've been smoking!" he accused. "No sh—, Dad" was the only answer I offered. I knew I was in trouble.

He ordered me upstairs to the bedroom and told me to take down my Levi's. "I'll go upstairs, but if you want my Levi's down, you'll have to take them down yourself," I retorted.

I waited with a mixture of fear and revulsion. Pretty soon Dad came in, pulling his two-inch-wide belt out of his trousers. He let me keep my pants on, but he thrashed me. He kept insisting that I would never smoke again. I kept saying, "I promise you I *will* learn to smoke, and I will smoke *forever!*" Finally Dad gave up in exhaustion.

I marched out of the house and hitchhiked into town. I bought a pack of Pall Malls, found a friend and asked him to teach me to smoke. I smoked for the next eight years.

That day marked the beginning of the end of my relationship with my father. I am sure that Dad reacted so forcefully because he thought he had already lost Frank and didn't want to lose me. (Frank had gotten himself kicked out of boarding school at age twelve and had joined the Marines at fifteen.)

I hated my father during those teen-age years. Our relationship became a series of confrontations, all unpleasant. He hated everything I did. Shortly after learning how to smoke, I had my first drink in a bar. Between seventh and eighth grades I had grown seven inches and gained fifty pounds. With a doctored draft card, I could pass for twenty-one. Pretty soon I was buying booze for my friends. I didn't go to school much, and on several occasions I simply disappeared from home for weeks or months at a time.

I rebelled against everything my parents stood for. As far as I could tell, they didn't like who I was. I certainly didn't want anything to do with who they were. My parents weren't bad people; on the contrary, they were dedicated Christians. They had been missionaries for more than twenty years. Nevertheless, my family was dysfunctional in many ways, failing to provide the nurture and security that children need in order to grow into healthy adults.

My parents took seriously the command to "seek first the kingdom of God." They believed this to mean that if they were faithful in pursuing their ministry, God would take care of the needs of their children. Family was last on their list of priorities, and as kids, we experienced this low commitment directly.

I was born among Tibetans in China, but by the time I was three my parents had returned home for furlough. And because of the Communist Revolution in China, they never went back there. They continued their active involvement in ministry, however. Through most of my childhood, we lived in a series of towns in New York State. My parents would go into a community where a church had been closed. They would find out who had the key and get permission to start a Sunday school. They would work there until the revived church could afford to hire a part-time pastor. Then they would turn the church over and begin the process all over again. They had Bible studies, classes and children's programs going every day of the week. As a youngster, I got dragged to most of them.

In many ways, though, my parents had never left Asia. They had lived with few material possessions among the Tibetans and saw no reason why they couldn't do without those things at home. Our clothes came from donations to church missionary barrels. The clothes were already well worn when they were given away, and as the fourth boy in the family, by the time I got a piece of clothing there wasn't much left.

I was embarrassed by my parents, their lifestyle and their commitment to ministry. The only time I remember willingly acknowledging that my parents were missionaries was in high school when I gave a report on Tibet. My dysfunctional family background left me with deep scars of insecurity, anger and weakness that made me wonder what I could ever contribute to society. What amazes me most about my life is that God took that wounded, rebellious young man and, even through my areas of greatest weakness, has been able to use my life to advance his kingdom.

Fifteen years ago, I had a chance to catch a free ride to Brazil with a friend who was a missionary pilot. Together we traveled around the country. My friend offered seminars for other mission pilots. At the time I was superintendent of children's education for Wycliffe Bible Translators, so I ran programs to encourage teachers and school administrators. The last night of our trip I was asked to speak to the teen-age students at the center in Tumichucua, Bolivia, situated on the edge of a beautiful lake. It was a pleasure to interact with them, but by the time the meeting ended, I was ready to get some sleep before our trip home the next morning.

"Mr. Harrison, have you got a minute?" asked the student walking out of the building with me. Jack Schumaker had a reputation as a fine Christian young man and a leader in the community. He wanted to talk and suggested we go down to the dock on the lake. Jack and I spent several hours together. Most of the time I listened to him. He told me that he was a hypocrite; he really didn't believe there was a God. He said he had never experienced an answer to prayer—and neither had his parents. I knew his parents were godly people, Bible translators who were being powerfully used among a tribal group in Bolivia, but I didn't argue with Jack. Instead, I told him a little about my background. In many ways he was very much like me, a missionary kid who didn't see the value in his parents' ministry, who didn't believe in the God they served. The only advice I gave him was to urge him to stick out his neck in faith, to ask God for something important to him.

We had been sitting by the beautiful moonlit lake, with only a few mosquitos to interrupt us. But suddenly, in the early morning hours, we heard a bloodcurdling scream from one of the homes above us. It was a baby screaming, it seemed for eternity. My first thought was that we should pray for that baby. My second thought was, "If you pray and nothing happens, Jack is going to think that you don't have any better connections with that God you talk about than he does." Inwardly hesitating, I encouraged Jack to pray. He said, "No, you pray."

"No, you pray," I insisted.

He started to pray, "Dear Lord . . . thank you for bringing Mr. Harrison here . . ." He couldn't seem to go any further.

I knew I had to pray for that baby. I asked God to put his hand on that child and bring peace into that home. The baby stopped screaming. Jack seemed surprised and delighted. We finished our conversation, and I went to bed for a couple of hours before flying off the next morning.

A few weeks later, I received a letter from Bolivia telling me the rest of the story. Jack had gone to the high school principal the next morning and asked to speak in chapel. "But Jack," the principal replied, "we have a program planned. You can speak some time in the future, perhaps in a few weeks."

"I can't wait until then," Jack insisted. "I have to say something to the students and the teachers. I have to do it today."

*17*

The principal wisely let him go ahead. In chapel Jack acknowledged his hypocrisy to the community, telling them what he had said to me. He went on to say that God worked a miracle before his eyes the previous night. He had committed his life to the Lord.

And it really was a miracle. I didn't know it at the time, but every night for the previous two and a half weeks that baby had woken up and screamed for thirty to forty-five minutes. The family had already decided to return to the United States because the local doctor had not been able to find a cause for the screaming. I'm glad I didn't know the circumstances because I probably wouldn't have had the faith to pray for the baby. What I told Jack that night was something that has been proven true in my experience any number of times: God responds to the tiniest steps of faith, often in surprising ways.

Early in 1989 my wife, Shelby, and I decided it was time to try to establish a crosscultural and academic exchange between American and Soviet students. We had worked with InterVarsity Christian Fellowship's missions division for two years and had seen a lot of success with a similar program in China. So, without a single appointment, we headed for Moscow.

When we reached our seat assignments on the New York-to-Moscow flight, we found that our seatmate was an experienced American diplomat who had just been assigned to the American embassy in Moscow. His job description included academic exchanges! He was able to introduce us to the man he was replacing—a man who had his finger on the pulse of the Soviet educational system and the changes arising out of *perestroika*. The advice we got in the embassy caused us to change our strategy, which considerably strengthened our negotiating position since we approached persons in the three

Soviet universities who were simply names to us.

All three universities were interested in our proposal; two of them agreed to begin the program that summer. One of the historic agreements we signed with those universities begins: "Kiev State University, in the spirit of Terovshevshenko [the poet laureate of the Ukraine], and the InterVarsity Christian Fellowship of the U.S. of A. do agree to the following..." When this was translated from Russian to English for me in the presence of the Soviet university delegation, the vice-rector commented, "You know, Mr. Harrison, we don't despise religion like we once did. Religious people, Christians, are often very solid citizens. They are dependable. Fewer of them suffer from alcoholism, and that's a real problem for us."

How did we know where to go, what to do, who to see in order to bring about that agreement? We didn't. We had sought advice and gathered as much information as we could, but in the end, we had to rely on our keen sense that it was time. We had to trust that God would use our risk-taking even beyond what we were expecting.

That simple principle I shared with Jack Schumaker and that Shelby and I claimed as we flew to Moscow has been a foundational and life-transforming truth for me. God responds to our acts of faith, no matter how small or feeble. It has been a long road from the angry, rebellious days of my adolescence to that trip to the Soviet Union, and the journey is continuing still. The road has been marked with tiny steps of faith—seeking help in overcoming the hurts of my past, obeying God in small ways, praying that he would use me in some way. The road has also been marked with surprising evidences of God's grace—healing and changed attitudes, restored relationships and unimagined opportunities. It is a journey that began in brokenness, which has had its share of pain as well as joy. It is a journey guided by a goal, a promise that I will be "made complete in Christ" (Col 2:10).

# 2

# *Crippled Children*

O ne day I asked my father if I could visit a friend in a nearby town. He said no. I asked why, and when the only answer he gave was, "Just because it's best," I got mad.

I went anyway. My friend lived on a farm, and I was eager to learn something about farming from him. We decided we would try out his father's tractor. I'm not sure he was allowed to drive the tractor himself, since we were only twelve. We set out up a steep hill near the barn. Suddenly the rear tires began to spin, and we felt the tractor sliding backwards, gaining speed as it rolled toward a stone wall. We slammed backward into the wall. My foot was caught behind the tailgate; my heel was virtually cut off.

I was in excruciating pain. Blood was spurting everywhere. My friend panicked, not knowing what to do. His parents took me to the hospital, where I had surgery on my foot and was put in a cast. My anger at my Dad's no and his refusal to tell me his reasons resulted in more than six weeks of hobbling around, a great deal of pain, and even some question over whether I would lose my foot.

As I grew up I sensed that some things weren't right about my family. It wasn't right that my father didn't express his love to me. It wasn't right that I grew up feeling that inadequate and insecure. Many years later, I realized that my family was dysfunctional.

My parents were married for more than forty years. They were respected members of the community, known as godly people who were dedicated to serving others. Our family didn't have some of the overt characteristics of a dysfunctional family, such as divorce, drug or alcohol abuse, or other compulsive behaviors. Some of the discipline my father exercised would probably be considered child abuse today, but on the outside, we seemed like a normal family.

Under the surface, though, we fit almost every category marking a dysfunctional family. Dysfunctional families tend to be characterized by a set of rigid, inhuman rules, while functional families have rules that are flexible and designed to meet the needs of the members of the family. In dysfunctional families communication is indirect: feelings are not expressed openly; certain subjects are never discussed; conflict is avoided at all costs. In functional families, members communicate openly and directly, working out their differences in an atmosphere of love and acceptance. Functional families provide an atmosphere of love and respect which helps children develop healthy self-esteem based on an accurate understanding of themselves. Dysfunctional families offer distorted reflections of the child: implicitly blaming the child for family problems, denying the child's worth through abuse or simply ignoring the child's need for love and nurture. Children in functional families feel secure and valued for themselves. Children in dysfunctional families find it difficult to trust people.

My parents believed that it was their responsibility to break their children's wills. Their authority was not to be questioned, and any infraction of their rules was met with harsh punishment.

My parents didn't discuss their feelings. I never saw them resolve conflict. We could hear their whispered arguments and feel the tension in the house but never knew if and how they settled their disagreements. If I got into a fight with one of my brothers, one or both of us would be punished for fighting; it didn't matter what the fight was about. We were taught to control our emotions, not to talk about them.

I had a terrible self-image as a teen-ager. I couldn't seem to succeed in school and was constantly criticized for my behavior and appearance. My parents wondered why I couldn't behave like some of my brothers (not Frank) and my sister. They couldn't control me, so they finally decided that maybe someone else could. After threatening to send me to boarding school, they sent me to live with one of my brothers and his wife.

For years I struggled with the crippling effects of my dysfunctional past. I was an insecure person, prone to critical words and outbursts of anger. I became a workaholic, driven to do everything and do it well, even at the risk of neglecting the needs of my family. I was repeating the cycle of destructive behavior that had marked my childhood. Only after many years of seeing God work at changing these things in my life did I begin to realize that these aspects of my character are typical of children from dysfunctional families of all types. As I began to learn more about the characteristics of adults who grew up in dysfunctional families, I recognized many aspects of myself.

Children in dysfunctional families develop certain coping mechanisms; in adulthood these usually have destructive consequences. Regardless of the nature of the family dysfunction, the children from these families share many characteristics. Sometimes they are referred to as "adult children," as in "adult children of alcoholics." The term *codependent* has also gained widespread use. It originally referred to people in close relationship with a substance abuser, who in some way participate in or enable the addict's behavior, but it has also been applied in a more general way to people who share the characteristics of dysfunctional family members.

"Adult children" have much in common, although their behavior may appear at one extreme of the spectrum or the other. They can be extremely irresponsible or hyper-responsible. They can be total conformists or utter rebels. They can be high achievers or dropouts from society. They can be extremely quiet, unemotional types or explosively angry people. They can seem self-assured to the point of arrogance or self-effacing to the point of invisibility. I started out as a rebel, but later found myself conforming too much to other people's expectations. Nevertheless, both behaviors were attempts to cope with the same underlying problems.

One of the dysfunctional family's rules, usually unspoken, is

"Don't feel." In one way or another, children are taught not to express their emotions. It is not uncommon, then, that as adults they find it difficult to acknowledge, identify or talk about feelings. Children who never hear their parents talk about feelings may grow up believing it is never appropriate to share emotions, or they may simply be unable to do so. As a child I never heard my father tell me that he loved me. For a long time after I was married, I found it impossible to say "I love you" to my wife.

Negative emotions are even harder for people in dysfunctional families to deal with. Anger in particular is a big issue for many adult children. In many respects, we have a lot to be angry about. We have often been victims of abuse or in some way have been deprived of healthy childhoods. But we don't know how to deal with anger in mature, healthy ways. Most of us have grown up in environments which taught us that the best thing to do with feelings is to act like we're not feeling them.

Emotions are physiological energy; they eventually get expressed, one way or another. Anger turned inward is a deadly force, leading to physical symptoms like ulcers or emotional ones like depression. Anger also breeds resentments and bitterness, which slowly but surely dominate our character and turn us into sour, negative people. And even when we've done our best to stuff our anger under the rug, it leaks out the sides, manifesting itself in sarcasm and other unintentionally harmful behavior.

Some have learned to use anger as a shield. Other people walk around them on tiptoes, afraid of setting off a torrent of angry words. They have no idea what action or comment might touch a point of insecurity and set off the big guns. This kind of anger is abusive and keeps others from getting too close.

Adult children of dysfunctional families tend to be controllers. They attempt to control themselves, circumstances, and other people, often through manipulation and deception. Frequently they had to take care of an alcoholic parent or in some other way assume adult responsibilities as a child. They tend to be motivated by a need to "take care of" people close to them, usually in a way that suffocates the person and creates an angry backlash.

Underneath this controlling behavior lies a problem that psychologists refer to as "weak boundaries." The term refers to an underdeveloped sense of where "I" end and "you" begin. They often feel responsible for other people's thoughts, feelings and actions. They worry obsessively about other people and their problems. Sometimes we find it hard to recognize that we aren't responsible for what someone else is feeling— and we let ourselves feel guilty about the prospect of disappointing someone. People-pleasing is a common trait of adult children, and it is rooted in this urge to make sure everyone else around us is feeling OK, even if we aren't.

As much as they find themselves driven by what they perceive to be other people's desires, adult children are also expert manipulators. We know how things are "supposed to be," and so we badger, criticize and manipulate others into conforming to our view of the universe. Guilt is usually the medium of exchange for these "transactions"; if we succeed in making the other person feel guilty, they will usually do what we want them to do.

This is false guilt or what we might call "unearned" guilt. It has nothing to do with what we feel when we have sinned or violated our own values. That kind of guilt leads to repentance and forgiveness, but false guilt is a prison where we give people power to control us or similarly attempt to control others.

Problems with self-esteem are characteristic of the children of dysfunctional families. Not having received clear messages from their parents which told them they were loved and valued as children, they find it difficult to accept their own worth independent of what they do or what others think of them. My parents tried to motivate me by telling me I could do better. If I brought home a C grade on my report card, they would say it should have been a B. They unwittingly communicated that I would never measure up, never earn their approval.

Perfectionism and workaholism are common traits that usually stem from this lack of healthy self-esteem. We are constantly trying to prove our worth by doing more things better and faster than others. We feel indispensable—no one else is quite as capable as we are—and sometimes we convince those around us that we are indispensable. They are often in the position of trying to work harder to make up for some perceived weakness. Insecurity drives an engine that sooner or later runs out of control.

For a perfectionist, everything is either a total, unqualified success or an abject failure. With such a fragile sense of one's own self-worth, failure is a thing to be avoided at all costs, but inevitably the perfectionist maneuvers himself into a place where failure is inevitable because the task is simply too great.

Perfectionism is also linked to the fact that dysfunctional families often have a rigid set of rules. The way to stay out of trouble in such a home was to adhere to the rules—if you could just obey them perfectly, you would have no more problems. In adulthood, the perfectionist thinks that "breaking the rules" or not living up to unreasonable expectations will result in disaster all out of proportion to the situation. This is an example of the kind of distorted thinking that is often part of codependence. Focusing on causes and effects and seeing those causes in an essentially self-centered way leads to all kinds of faulty conclusions. The wife of an alcoholic might think that if she keeps the house perfectly clean, her husband will quit drinking. She can't see that those things aren't related at all.

Another major trait of adult children is denial. Denial is the first stage of grief, a natural reaction to pain or loss of any kind. A child's shattering realization that his parents are not perfect—that they are in fact deeply troubled, negligent or abusive—is met first with denial. In a dysfunctional family, the child doesn't have an opportunity to talk through this sense of loss. His means of coping with it is simply to pretend the problem isn't there.

Denial becomes a habit, and adult children have a hard time accepting reality, from the inner reality of their own emotions to the fact that they cannot control everything and everyone they come in contact with. They spend a lot of energy hiding reality from themselves and others. They deny their pain; they deny the nature of their problems; they deny themselves. They accept lies as truth, whether they hear them from an addicted loved one or from one's own twisted thinking. Ann Wilson Schaef has written in *Co-Dependence: Misunderstood—Mistreated,* "An addiction is anything we feel we have to lie about." Truth is devalued, something to be feared instead of a source of freedom. Denial means you aren't free.

In many people these coping mechanisms produce progressively more disabling effects. Lethargy, depression and even suicidal tendencies can appear, as well as serious physical and mental illness. Frequently adult children of dysfunctional families are trying to do the impossible: keep the world, themselves and those they love under control. Eventually the strain of trying to play God wears them out. Under this stress, such people run a high risk of developing compulsive habits such as eating disorders, alcohol or drug addiction and sexual or physical abuse.

As a condition that has its origin in family dynamics, codependence is almost inevitably passed on to the next generation. Adult children from dysfunctional families often have no other pattern for raising their own children. Their families become dysfunctional and their children develop the same kinds of problems—"the sin of the fathers to the third and fourth generation" (Num 14:18). Given this tendency, all the evidence points to an increasing percentage of young people in our society who will face the enduring consequences of growing up in dysfunctional families.

Since the early 1980s there have been more than one million divorces each year in the United States, involving at least a million children annually. The average marriage that ends in divorce lasts seven years, and demographers predict that in the 1990s seventy per cent of the population will come from broken homes.

Around twelve million Americans are alcoholics, each one of them having a negative impact on an average of at least four people around them, including an estimated fifteen million children. Nearly half of those who grow up with an alcoholic parent will eventually marry an alcoholic themselves. By the age of sixteen, one out of four girls has been sexually abused. Eating disorders afflict sixty per cent of the women in America and half of all men.

The number of single-parent families has grown by fifty per cent since 1970. More and more of these families are headed by women living below the poverty line, increasing the level of stress and potential for dysfunction. Violence is a characteristic of some fifteen million families. Anne Wilson Schaef reports that some theorists in the field claim that codependence applies in one degree or another to nearly everyone in our society: it's a cultural syndrome and part of our society's generally addictive approach to life.

The Christian community is not exempt from the problems of dysfunctional families, as my experience indicates. The increasing number of Christian young people who come from dysfunctional homes, whether their parents were Christian or not, raises an important question for those of us concerned about fulfilling the Great Commission. Not too long ago, I heard the head of a mission agency say, "If more than half of today's college students come from dysfunctional backgrounds, we cannot send dysfunctional persons to the mission field to sort out their problems."

I took issue with him, not because I want to see more stressed-out missionaries but because of the implication that mission agencies have no responsibility to help potential missionaries through the healing process. I have been a missions administrator so I understand that resources are limited and that agencies would rather deal with people who seem to have their lives together. But I wonder where I would have ended up if someone had applied that standard to me.

It is important to deal with the issues of the past and look carefully at the way the hurts and disappointments of yesterday affect my life and witness today, but I wouldn't disqualify anyone on the basis of a dysfunctional background. That's like putting limits on God. God delights in using unpromising material —my life is testimony to that fact, as are many other examples from the Bible and history.

Brokenness is not a permanent condition. Much of my healing has happened in the context of living out my commitment to serve God in the world. He has used fellow missionaries, students I was teaching and, most of all, my wife and children to work healing and transformation in my life. I am convinced that what the world needs more than ever is missionary servants who offer good news rooted in their own experience of God's healing love, not people who "have their act together" but don't know how to identify with the brokenhearted people Jesus wants to touch.

# 3

# *Second Chances*

B y the time I was fifteen years old I had quit school four or five times. After the last time, my brother Frank and I disappeared from Ithaca, where my parents were living, and headed for Augusta, Georgia. On our way out of town, we heard on the radio that a car had been stolen. We thought we'd be blamed for it, so we decided to change our names.

In Augusta the O'Hare brothers soon were established in town. Frank lied about his age and got a job selling insurance. He told me to find a job in a gas station, which I did. But I didn't like the fact that I was working long, hard hours, while he wore a suit and came home with his fingernails clean. I decided I would get into the insurance business too.

The salesperson who had taught Frank to sell thought that if one O'Hare brother was good, two would certainly be better. In the course of three months, my brother went to the top of the company, and I was tenth in sales. We promoted insurance to everyone we came in contact with. Sometimes our eagerness for a sale put us into conflict. I didn't mind making up stories and manipulating people into buying insurance, but I tried to be fair and not sell them more than they could afford. Frank, on the other hand, would sell as much as he could, and then I had to pick up the pieces with some of his customers. We lived a fast, exciting life there, but I wasn't entirely happy.

I began to date a girl who worked in one of the restaurants we frequented. She was nice and attractive, and soon I was falling in love with her. That's when my fast life in Georgia started to unravel. Our relationship was founded on sand: I had lied to her about my name, my age, my background, nearly everything about me. After a while I couldn't live with those lies any more. Something had survived of all that my parents had drilled into me: basic values like honesty and integrity were ingrained in me and I couldn't live in conflict with them for long.

Finally, I told Joyce the truth. It was the end of our friendship but an important turning point for me. Soon afterward, I wrote my mother a letter, the first in six months. I told her I was coming home. I was going to finish high school and go on to college.

I was in for a rude awakening. I was a kid again, after six months of working, making money and driving around in a brand new car. I had attended school a total of forty-five days my tenth-grade year, and the only way I could get a diploma was to major in shop. I wasn't a success in school, but I graduated. I wanted to go on to college, but where?

That summer my parents brought home a catalog from a small Christian college in Tennessee called Bryan College. In big type across the cover were the words "Christ above all." That wasn't what I was looking for, and as I leafed through the list of rules and regulations I knew why. But my mother gently reminded me of that catalog a couple of times. "You know, you might be able to get into that school," she suggested.

I thought she might be right. I wrote a letter to the president: Dear Mr. President, I'm not a Christian. I smoke and drink. I notice you've got a lot of rules. I won't promise to keep them. But I'll try. I really do want to get an education, and besides, I'm a missionary kid. (I thought if I had a trump card, I might as well use it.)
The president, Dr. Mercer, wrote back and said he wanted me to come.

As soon as I stepped on campus, Dr. Mercer called me into his office. He closed the door and said, "Now, young man, you and I know a lot about your past. I want you to know that no one else on this campus knows. Furthermore, you're in a school where the teachers are Christians. They care a lot about their students. They will help you. And you're going to need help.

"God made you an intelligent person," he added. "Why not let this be the beginning of a totally different life for you? Why not allow the beautiful person that God made you to be flourish here? Don't let the past handicap you." I had never had anyone tell me something like that before. I was all set for a message like, "Harrison, we're going to be watching you." It was a demonstration of grace, and that was just the beginning of my experience at Bryan.

The dean, Dr. Bartlett, called me in next. "I don't know much about your background," he said, "but one of the students told me that you had been out in the work world. Well, you'll find this college has a lot of rules. I don't expect you to keep them all, but I'm going to make two requests of you when you break one. First, don't tell your friends. Second, come tell me."

I didn't break as many rules as I might have, and I always told Dr. Bartlett. He never condemned me. He would ask me if I enjoyed doing whatever I had done or if I was going to do it again. But I knew he accepted me no matter what I had done.

The students at Bryan were another challenge to all my stereotypes of Christians. A number of them reached out to me. I was suspicious at first, but I soon saw that they were genuinely loving people. I had strong convictions that were quite the opposite of what my parents had taught me, but they were based on stereotypes of Christians as negative, judgmental people, people who didn't smoke, didn't drink, didn't do any of the things I liked to do. When I started to see accepting, gracious, loving Christians who knew how to have fun and enjoy themselves, my stereotypes were shattered and my conviction that I didn't want to be a Christian crumbled. I knew that all the things I'd been taught as a child were true, and now I wanted to follow Christ. One day, after chapel, my roommate prayed with me as I committed my life to the Lord.

I spent two years at Bryan. I found the Lord there. I met my wife there. In a lot of ways I found myself there. I could hardly believe it when I achieved anything, but at Bryan I found myself doing a lot of things I didn't think I'd ever be able to do.

Shelby convinced me to take a course in her major, which was one of the toughest classes in the school. I got an A. I developed relationships with some of my professors, and their respect for me helped me to think about myself in new ways. I decided I could be myself there. Shelby and I got involved in the Student Foreign Mission Fellowship there, stimulating our interest in missions.

Another important mentor in these transitional years was Professor Wilcox, a retired professor from Cornell University. When I got back from Georgia, my parents were living in his house in Ithaca, and my mother was taking care of him. I had never known anyone like him. He was 97 when I first met him but read a book a day. He walked one to six miles every day. Every meal was an intellectually stimulating experience. (He kept a big unabridged dictionary next to the table, and we consulted it at least once per meal.)

Professor Wilcox was the first person I can recall who interacted with me as if I had something meaningful to contribute to the conversation. He helped me believe in my ability to succeed in college. When I grew interested in anthropology and sociology, which were subjects Bryan didn't offer, he encouraged me to transfer to Cornell.

Professor Harden interviewed me for Cornell. It took about five hours, and all the time his reception room was full of people. He kept asking me for my high-school transcript. I had given him my transcript from Bryan, but I didn't want him to see my high-school record.

Eventually he insisted. When he looked at it rather late in our interview, he was shocked. "Joseph," he said, using my first name, "that has got to be the worst high school transcript I have ever seen!" I'm sure it was. At the end of the interview he shook his head. "Everything in your record indicates that you will fail at Cornell," he said. "I can't imagine why I'm doing this, but I'm going to let you in." He proceeded to transfer all but ten semester hours from Bryan.

Cornell was an exciting place to be. This was the early sixties, and Shelby and I got involved with events on campus. We demonstrated and marched. Like other students of our generation we were out to change the world. We were involved with an InterVarsity chapter and prayer meetings where we prayed for concerns all over the world. We also got involved in a church where I was discipled by the pastor. But the most important thing that happened during those three years was the reconciliation between my father and me.

Our wedding symbolized my changing attitudes toward my family. We were married in Shelby's home church in Texas, but my entire family was able to attend. It was the first time we were all together in fifteen years—and the last ever, as it turned out. All three of my brothers stood up with me, and my father performed the ceremony. It was very moving, given the level of alienation that had existed between us just a few years earlier. Even after the wedding, Shelby and I spent a few days in town, enjoying the family reunion.

The healing of my relationship with my father didn't happen all at once. While I was at Cornell, Shelby and I lived in an apartment in the attic of my parents' house, and I would normally have lunch with my parents. Many days we would continue our conversation well into the afternoon, and there were times I worried that I should be studying instead of talking with my Dad.

We argued a lot—I was a hot-shot Ivy League student, and I thought I knew it all. The longer I was around Cornell, the more liberal my thinking about politics became. I wasn't very tolerant of my father's politics; he "always voted for the man, never the party," but the men he voted for were always Republicans.

A lot of healing happened in those times, despite our arguments. We talked about some of my childhood experiences, and, without being defensive, my parents explained their point of view—why they had decided to go without certain things. They told me stories of their experiences in China, and I found my respect and admiration for them growing.

We became more able to express love and affirmation to one another. At first my father was more demonstrative with Shelby than with me, but he would respond to my efforts to hug him. I don't remember the event of asking for my father's forgiveness, but I know I asked him because I had hurt him in many ways. During that period of time, my bitterness and hatred toward him were gone. The Lord took care of it. In fact, I became his defender with others in the family. They hadn't experienced what I had—that sense of forgiveness and reconciliation.

In 1963 my parents celebrated their fortieth anniversary. We organized a big surprise party for them at my brother's church. Shelby and some friends cooked a gourmet Chinese meal. It was Shelby's idea to give them wedding bands as a present. They had bands when they were married, but my father's had worn out, and my mother had put hers in the offering a couple of years after they were married. (It was during a famine in China, and people were dying all around them.) We were able to say some things to them that evening to express our love. It was a very healing time.

As my graduation neared, Shelby and I began to consider our

future. We had an interest in missions from the beginning but were trying to discover where God wanted us to serve. We talked to representatives from various missions agencies but felt that we wouldn't fit into their structures. I had some ideas about helping missionaries be more strategic and a concern for some of the family problems I'd experienced. The mission representatives would just laugh when I started to talk about these unconventional ideas.

Then the policies of most missions got in the way. I felt I couldn't fulfill my God-given responsibility to my own family, especially when we had children, under their policies about finances and children. I wasn't about to join a mission where a missionary's children were not really considered part of ministry. I was against missionary boarding schools—as ironic as that would turn out to be. So we were aiming for what is now known as tentmaking—planning to teach in a university somewhere in Asia.

While we were going through this process, we made some friends who were missionaries with Wycliffe Bible Translators. They didn't strike up a friendship in order to recruit us, but they encouraged our interest in the mission. Gradually I discovered that Wycliffe's policies were not what I had expected. One day, they came over to our house with a letter from Papua New Guinea telling about an urgent need for teachers for their high school for missionary kids at the center in Ukarumpa. We seemed to be exactly what they needed, and the more we considered it, the more the Lord seemed to be leading us in that direction.

But first, I wanted to get my father's input before making a definite decision. Shelby and I went to Dad, and I said, "Shelby and I feel like the Lord wants us with Wycliffe, and we've been praying about that possibility. But before we move forward, we want your blessing." My Dad was never one to respond spontaneously. If you asked his advice, he would go and pray about it and then let you know what he thought about it. But that day, he immediately took us into his arms and blessed us, praying for us. I was amazed and overwhelmed. That moment of experiencing his approval and enthusiasm for our plans and for us is a memory I'll always treasure.

My Dad died within five months of my graduation. I felt like I had been robbed, but I am forever grateful for those three years of reconciliation and healing we experienced.

That summer Shelby and I headed off for the Summer Institute of Linguistics, Wycliffe's training program. After getting some teaching experience and earning a master's degree, we were on our way to Papua New Guinea. The "high school" we were supposed to teach in consisted of twenty-eight students following twelve different correspondence courses. I determined that we could offer those missionary kids more than that, and began to develop our own program. Within six months I became headmaster of the school. Four years later, on our first furlough, I was asked to establish a children's education department for Wycliffe worldwide. I was superintendent for all of Wycliffe's schools while continuing to work in the Ukarumpa High School. During this time my family responsibilities were expanding—three of our four daughters were born in Papua New Guinea.

The second chances that God offered me in my early adult years were formative experiences for me. Through people who believed in me and were willing to take a chance on me, I started to turn my life around. But achieving the dream of serving God in missions was only the beginning of the story.

*41*

I experienced a lot of changes in my life from my wild teen years, but there were plenty more to come. God had begun the process of turning my weaknesses into strengths, but the real challenges were still ahead. In those early years of serving in Papua New Guinea I began to face up to some of the vestiges of my dysfunctional family background, especially in dealing with criticism, anger, workaholism, guilt and the need to forgive.

# 4

# *From Criticism*
# *to*
# *Affirmation*

O n one of my earlier disappearances from home, when I was fourteen, I decided to take a bus to Daytona Beach, Florida, where Frank was living with his new wife. I borrowed the bus fare from my father and headed south. Frank and Patty already had a baby, and their tiny apartment was cramped with an extra person. Still, they welcomed me, and I felt accepted by them. They had big plans, including moving to California where my sister Beth and her family lived.

We piled into their dilapidated car with bald tires and a knocking rod in the engine and headed west. In California, I received a letter from my Dad. I tore the envelope open in my excitement. Most of the letter reminded me of my debts to Dad, including the bus fare. He asked me how I intended to pay it back. He was critical of me, saying I was a bit irresponsible. But he signed the letter, "Love, Dad."

*Love, Dad!* My Dad loved me! I hadn't known that, but he said so here, in writing! He must have loved me before. He still loved me, even though I owed him money. I carried that letter in my wallet until it wore out and I could no longer read "Love, Dad."

From birth until adulthood, I do not remember my father telling me at any other time that he loved me. What I heard and experienced from him was criticism, harsh discipline and disapproval. I didn't sense his love and respect, and in turn found it hard to respect him.

Again, my parent's lifestyle was a constant source of embarrassment to me. They were frugal to a fault, living well below what they could have afforded even on their small income. Long before the idea became popular, my father had an organic garden. He thought it built character to spend time weeding the garden. I considered it pure drudgery, which I always resisted and resented. He bought a couple of goats but soon we had seventeen of them. I had the privilege of looking after them too.

I didn't respect people who kept goats. I didn't respect people who could afford something new and wouldn't buy it. I didn't respect people who sacrificially spent all their time, energy and resources sharing the gospel. I was embarrassed by the tracts that my parents left at every gas station and every restaurant. I didn't respect the very high, perhaps rigid, standards my parents kept regarding Christian separation from the world. As I approached my teens, the idea that I was different from my peers because of my parents' way of life became a very painful reality, a source of insecurity that I tried to hide with my rebellion.

My parents didn't believe in television, so I went to the neighbors' house and watched theirs. My father refused to pay for barbershop haircuts—he figured the difference between a good haircut and a bad one was about a week. In my eyes, most of them were bad, so the first money I earned at age twelve was spent on a real haircut. We didn't waste money on new clothes, so whatever money I earned from my first job went to buy clothes and shoes.

By the time I was a teen-ager I was spending most of my time away from home. I seemed to find more acceptance and affirmation in other people's homes or out with my friends. I had a friend named Paul whose parents thought the sun rose and set with me. "If Paul's with Danny, he's OK," they would say. My parents thought about the same of Paul. We got into plenty of trouble together! My friends were a refuge, but no one who was truly significant to me was telling me I was OK or even that I had potential.

It wasn't just my parents who criticized me and helped me to think of myself as a failure. When I decided to come home from Georgia and finish high school, the reaction of one of my brothers was typical: "Ha! He'll never finish high school, much less college." Obviously he and everyone else expected me to fail. I didn't feel I belonged in a family where almost everyone had gone to college.

The feedback I got at school was mostly negative. I was the night manager at a gas station and always had grease under my fingernails. Teachers would comment on my dirty hands or tight jeans or long hair. No one bothered to tell me I had a brain and should use it.

As a result, "insecurity" seems like such a puny word to describe the depths of despair that I have felt about myself at times. I was deeply ashamed of myself, I felt hopeless. It wasn't the kind of despair that leads to suicide, but it immobilized me. Whatever I was asked to do I felt sure that I couldn't do. For example, one day at Bryan College I was asked to read the Bible in chapel. I was scared to death to stand in front of the whole school and read. Shelby told me later that she thought the veins in my neck would explode, so much blood had rushed into my face. I had learned to read when I was four, and as a preschooler I would read the King James Bible out loud to anyone who would listen to me, undaunted by the difficult names. But that confidence in my own abilities had been crushed by years of criticism.

My insecurity and fear of rejection influenced all my relationships, especially dating. As a teen I always looked for someone who would be willing to go steady with me right away. I clung to that girl, needing the security that comes from always having a date.

I decided to try to "be myself" at Bryan College after becoming a Christian. I would muster my courage and sit with a different group of five girls at each meal. (We had formal, sit-down meals.) I asked many different girls for dates, not being concerned with Hollywood standards of beauty. Eventually I developed a reputation of being a Romeo, who would build a girl up, form a relationship and then break her heart.

One day the guys in my dorm were complaining that they were bored. There was nothing to do and no one to date. "Baloney," I said. "There are girls on campus just waiting for you to call. Here's a dime. Make a call; make a date."

I started pushing them, and pretty soon they turned on me: "We bet you can't get a date with Skinner."

"Skinner" was Shelby Skinner, a beautiful young woman who had the reputation of doing everything right. She made straight A's; she was a dean's assistant; she never broke a rule. Furthermore, she was a junior and I was a lowly freshman, still new on campus. But I couldn't resist the dare. I picked up the phone and asked her for a date on Friday night. It wasn't until I hung up that I realized I already had a date for that night—with her roommate. I got a buddy to double date with me. I started the evening with the roommate and ended up with Shelby. That was the beginning of the end of my dating around. I fell hard. After dating for eighteen months Shelby and I married.

Shelby has been an instrument of healing and recovery in my life, but meeting her and getting married did not erase the scars of the earlier criticism I had lived with. I found it easy to be critical of everything and everyone, including her. My natural inclination is to criticize the one shoe out of place, not even seeing the nineteen that are in place. I thought that I would feel all right if only other people would conform. Shelby always gave the impression of having everything together, and if I ever saw a flaw in her, I jumped all over it. I tended to pick on her, criticizing all kinds of things, as if somehow I could make her over into some fictional ideal of the perfect wife— a non-existent person that I'm sure I wouldn't have liked if she did exist.

At one point on our first furlough from Papua New Guinea, Shelby was going through a difficult period of doubt. We were somewhat worn-out from our first four and a half years on the mission field, and she was beginning to wonder if God really cared about us and our family. Her doubts went straight to my core of insecurity. After all, I was convinced that she knew the Bible better than me. If she was doubting God's goodness, where did that leave me? I wasn't very supportive of her in that crisis, and that was part of a larger pattern of not affirming and accepting her for who she was, encouraging her to become the unique and beautiful person God made her to be.

Shortly after we returned to Papua New Guinea, another missionary couple shared with us some teaching they had received about the healing of memories. They had just adopted a two-year-old boy who had been waking up every night with terrible nightmares. One night they prayed over him, asking God to heal his memories and relieve him of this torment. The nightmares ended.

After hearing their story, Shelby and I invited them to pray for us. In the weeks before this I would sit in the back of the church, see the backs of my colleagues' heads (almost everyone there was a fellow missionary) and mentally critique them. I was hard on the teachers in the school and the students alike. I was especially critical of my family.

I saw the difference the next Sunday. A friend of mine was preaching, actually reading his sermon, which is something I would normally criticize. I recall sitting in the back of the church, and instead of thinking critically about the people I saw, I rejoiced over them and prayed for them.

My memories were not gone, but the hurt and insecurity that had resulted from those incidents were being healed. Gradually I found myself more accepting and less critical in other situations. I found myself more secure and less willing to criticize Shelby.

The Lord was showing me other ways to deal with the insecurity that haunted me in my early ministry. I had a tendency to compensate for insecurity with a certain kind of arrogance—the sense that I knew how to do things better than others. I was critical of the way things were done, trying to fix things or prove I could do it better. At the same time I had very little experience and often didn't really know what I was doing. As headmaster of the school I longed for praise and affirmation. My supervisor, Al Pence, was also new in his responsibilities as branch director. Nevertheless, he made a point of affirming me, especially in public. Whenever we had a school concert, which would be entertainment for the entire community, he would stand up at the end of the evening and affirm the school and thank me for my leadership. I had never experienced such open affirmation, but it became something I decided to do for people around me.

I knew I needed affirmation, but I wasn't sure how to ask for it appropriately. It was easier for me to see and respond to that need in others. In the school in Ukarumpa there were a couple of students through whom I learned valuable lessons about the power of affirmation.

One of these students was a sixteen-year-old who was a failure at everything. He wasn't a discipline problem, but he couldn't do anything right. He wet the bed regularly. He was hopeless in sports. The year before I arrived in Papua New Guinea, he had been given the award for the Person Who Tried Hardest. When I heard about that prize I was infuriated—instinctively I knew that the real message behind the award was, "You tried hard, but you didn't succeed at anything." Although I was never quite the total failure that this boy was, it wasn't hard for me to identify with his frustration and the inner rage

I'm sure he must have felt.

One day his parents invited us to dinner. In the course of preparing the meal, the parents began to discuss the differences between this boy and his older sister, right in front of them. "Now the eldest child, she is such a joy to us. She does well in school, as you know. She's so popular. Now our poor son, he's a nice child. It's too bad that he is so slow. We don't understand where his slowness comes from. He's just never been able to do school work. As a matter of fact he has difficulty with a lot of things."

I was shocked. I couldn't believe these parents were comparing their kids—and doing it in their presence and ours. I couldn't stand it. I wanted to confront them right there, but I managed to restrain myself, abruptly changing the subject. At the end of the evening, I invited the parents to come and see me in my office.

They came the next morning. I was nervous about what I was going to say, but I felt I had to do it. I knew how important the affirmation of people like Professor Wilcox and Dr. Mercer had been to me, and I could see what their lack of affirmation was doing to this kid. I tried to explain that each of us can only rise to the level of the expectations of people who are significant to us. When our parents think we're dumb, we believe they're right and act that way.

I suggested an experiment, and they were eager to participate. I suggested that they look for some brand new activity that he had never attempted before. They chose driving. Then, I said, look for one thing to affirm in the first driving experience. Even if he has a great deal of difficulty in getting started, don't criticize him. Simply affirm some quality, some progress. Begin to affirm other things along the way, and use only affirmation in teaching him to drive.

This boy became an excellent driver. Pretty soon he began to do better in school. He never made the honor role, but each grading period he moved up one grade, from F to D, from D to C. He didn't become an Olympic athlete, but he was able to participate more in sports, had a good attitude and was actually improving.

Years later when we were living in Dallas we met this guy's boss at church. He was working for a large accounting firm. His boss said, "He's an unusual young man, but he is absolutely brilliant. He can solve problems that stump everyone else in the office, even people with more education and experience."

Brin was another student who seemed to specialize in getting into trouble. The teachers wanted to talk about him at every faculty meeting. They asked me more than once to expel him because they were so frustrated with him.

I was praying about Brin one day, and it dawned on me that we teachers should think about the good qualities in Brin, as Paul teaches in Philippians: "Whatever is true, whatever is noble, whatever is right, whatever is pure, whatever is lovely, whatever is admirable—if anything is excellent or praiseworthy—think about such things" (Phil 4:8). We should encourage him and build him up. It sounded to me like a brilliant idea.

My teachers hated it. But they agreed to look for something to affirm in Brin. I was confident it wouldn't be hard, but after several days, not one of his teachers had found anything to affirm in Brin.

I asked the Lord to help me and decided to sit through one or two of Brin's classes myself. I sat through seven classes before I saw anything worth affirming. In the last class of the day, a girl in the class had embarrassed herself by spilling her books and papers all over the floor in front of the whole class. Brin eagerly helped her pick them up.

At the faculty meeting that afternoon, I told the faculty what I had seen and affirmed in Brin and encouraged them to affirm him too. I went to my office and called Brin's father. "Oh, no," was his first response, "what has Brin done now?" I quickly said, "No, it's nothing like that. He's not in trouble. I just wanted you to know I am proud of Brin for acting kindly." He couldn't believe his ears. Was I talking about his son?

As soon as Brin's mother got home, the father told her about the call. And when Brin came home his father said, "The headmaster called today." Brin was braced for a rebuke. "Mr. Harrison happened to see what you did for that girl at school today. He appreciated it and called us to tell us so." Brin was amazed I had even noticed. I had even called his parents. What was the big deal?

After that things began to change for Brin. Gradually he began to do other things that were positive. His grades improved. Soon he was on the honor roll. He became a very solid citizen at Ukarumpa High School.

This principle of thinking of the positive qualities of a person has become a powerful instrument of healing in our family as well. Several years ago a missionary home on furlough called me out of the blue. We were good friends with this man and his wife, who had been very helpful to us in the past, but we hadn't heard from them for some time. He said he and his wife were going to be passing through Dallas and asked if we would be home. I looked at my calendar and saw it was full. I told him, "Well, we haven't seen you for a long time, and you don't come our way very often. So if there is no flexibility in your schedule, I'll just clear those days." As soon as I hung up, I could see from Shelby's face that she was not at all pleased that I had invited them. Shelby is one of the most hospitable people I have ever met. She makes our home a welcome landing spot for all sorts of people from all over the world. There was obviously something else going on here.

It happened that a number of years previously Shelby and the girls had stayed with this couple while I was doing some extensive traveling. This man seemed to be going through a difficult period in his life, and everything Shelby did was wrong—the way she disciplined the children, how she ate, the choices she made. They were all wrong. He picked at her for most of the time I was gone. Shelby is a very delicate flower, and she didn't need the criticism and condemnation that she experienced during those days. She wasn't at all eager to see this man again and have them stay with us.

I tried feebly to persuade her to think positively about the opportunity. It didn't work. I was in a quandry. How was I going to un-invite these folks? And yet how could I not, given Shelby's strong feelings?

That was when I thought of Philippians 4:8. I suggested that we sit down and make a list of the qualities we appreciated in this couple, the things we loved in them. Shelby was not enthusiastic. Being a cooperative, loving person, however, she agreed to try. I had to come up with the first few items on the list, but before long Shelby was piping in—and she contributed more than I did. We ended up with a legal-size page, full on both sides with admirable qualities we recognized in this man and woman. By the time we had finished our list Shelby's dread of their visit was gone.

The evening these missionaries came, Shelby made a wonderful meal. We had a number of extra people at the table and I sat at one end of the long table and the man at the other. Well into the meal I explained that in anticipation of their visit Shelby and I had made a list of the qualities we appreciated and loved in this couple. I said we wanted to share this with them in the presence of our family so they could understand how much we loved them. I called them by name, looked them in the eye and said, "We love you because . . . We appreciate you for . . ." Part way down the list this man began to weep, and the tears ran off his chin. His wife was a little more controlled, but I could tell it touched her as well.

When we finished dinner and got up from the table, the first thing the man did was hug Shelby. Before the evening was over, he had hugged her three or four times. Not a word had gone between them about the trouble that had provoked Shelby's negative response to their coming, but that relationship had been healed. Later on, the man said that was the most wonderful experience in his entire life!

Learning to give and receive affirmation has been an important part of my recovery, and the most important affirmation any of us can receive is the kind that comes from God. Understanding and experiencing the depth of God's love for me and my family has been incredibly healing. Sometimes the most powerful reminders of his love have come in the most difficult situations.

One Saturday morning when we were living in Ukarumpa, we woke up to a frightening situation. We had had a party for the high school students the night before and had somehow neglected to clean up a bowl of peanuts. Paula, who was four, discovered them and was quietly munching away. (The kids were good about letting us sleep in on Saturdays.) Nineteen-month-old Melody got up too, and she wanted some peanuts. Paula hesitated, thinking that perhaps Melody was too young for peanuts, but Melody was becoming more insistent. Not wanting to wake us up, Paula gave in. By then Melody was angry, and she choked and inhaled a peanut or two.

I turned Melody upside down, pounded on her back. Finally air began passing through her windpipe as we took her to our missionary doctor. The doctor sent us on to the local hospital where he assured us they could remove the peanut with an X-ray and a bronchioscope. But that hospital didn't have the equipment for Melody, so they sent us to another one five hours drive away. Our World-War-2 jeep blew a tire on the way, but we made it. The surgeon there had a bronchioscope, though we later learned it was an adult-sized instrument and shouldn't have been used on a young child. At that point he also did a tracheotomy, inserting a breathing tube in Melody's throat.

He told us we needed to go to the capital, Port Moresby. The doctor there was able to remove the peanut—God had miraculously dislodged it from her lung. But Melody wasn't out of danger yet. The normal passageway was swollen shut, so the trachea tube couldn't be removed. After two weeks in Port Moresby the doctor had given up.

The next logical step was to take Melody to a hospital in one of the larger cities in Australia. Our director back in Ukarumpa encouraged us to go ahead and not to worry about the expense. He assured us that our colleagues were praying for Melody. The doctors in Sydney examined her, and within an hour they had more diagnostic information than we were able to get in two weeks in Papua New Guinea. However, their conclusion was no more encouraging; they predicted she might be in intensive care for six to eight months. Miraculous-ly, we left that hospital with Melody just ten days later.

We were full of gratitude to God for healing her and helping us through that scary time, but it was a couple of years later that we discovered just how wonderfully our Father was caring for us in those days. I was back in Australia, this time in Ade-laide. The Wycliffe representative there, Ken Bradshaw, met me at the airport. "Is this your first time in Aussie?" he asked. No, I'd been there before. "Were you down on holiday?" he asked. No, it wasn't a holiday. My nineteen-month-old baby inhaled a peanut, I explained. "We prayed for you!" he exclaimed.

I had to take hold of something, I was so surprised. This man, whom I had never heard of, and who had never heard of me, had prayed for Melody. It was inconceivable to me that such a complete stranger would pray for my child.

Later that evening I was in the Bradshaw's home, talking to some teachers about the joys and trials of ministering to mis-sionary kids. In the middle of the meeting there was a tele-phone call. Someone was calling from Papua New Guinea ask-ing them to pray for Carol Anderson, a new missionary who was in the hospital, gravely ill. We stopped our meeting and prayed for Carol.

At the end of the meeting, Marilyn Bradshaw got up quietly and went over to the phone. She opened the drawer and pulled out a list as long as my arm. She started telephoning people, repeating the same basic message: "Pray for Carol An-derson." She called a church, a prayer group, a parent's group, another church. I began to understand what had happened to Melody—hundreds of people had prayed for her.

That experience taught me so much about God's love. It was like God was saying to me, "This is something you need to understand: I am a big God, and this family of mine loves one another. They care about one another's pain and joy." It was a wonderful way for God to say I love you, I love your child. Having known an earthly father who couldn't articulate his love to me, this was a powerful experience. Despite my deeply felt insecurities, the reality of God's acceptance of me offered the freedom to live a life characterized by acceptance and affirmation of others.

# 5

# *From Anger*
# *to*
# *Forgiveness*

oy, you are going to get into big trouble! And when you do, don't call on me."

That was my father's reaction to my pride and joy— a 1949 Ford that I had bought against his wishes and had conned my girlfriend's father into licensing for me. I was fifteen and didn't have a driver's license, but I had earned the money to buy that car and was determined to drive it.

And I did. My gang of drinking buddies and I cruised the town, and when we were drunk, I'd usually be the one to drive, since they thought I would drive fairly sensibly even under the influence. Things swung along pretty well for a few months, and then someone decided to turn me in.

I was driving through the city of Ithaca one day when I saw the lights of the police car behind me. I pulled over. The next thing I knew I was in jail. The sheriff walked me into the cell block, opened the door and made some remark about lunch in an hour or two. I looked around the cell, and there was Frank. He had run out of money and tried to pawn some furniture he was buying on time. I told him how I was nabbed, and we whiled away our time gambling our slices of bread.

My sentence for driving without a license was fifty dollars or thirty days. I didn't have the money, so I called my Dad. True to his word, he refused to talk to me. If there was any time in my life I thought I needed my Dad, it was then. He wouldn't even let my mother help me; she was a soft touch and I knew I could get her to bail me out.

Thirty days in jail would mean not finishing the school year, which would probably result in my expulsion and admittance to reform school, where some of my friends were already "enrolled." I saw my life going downhill quickly, but my father wasn't lifting a finger to help me. Eventually my girlfriend and some other friends pitched in and got me out, but the anger and rage I felt toward my father was nearly overwhelming.

Anger became a trademark of my behavior in my teen years, and it had increasingly destructive consequences. In ninth grade I flunked algebra: I was making B's and C's on the tests, but because I refused to do homework, the teacher failed me. Several members of my gang ended up in a summer-school class with me that summer. The teacher had just finished his first year of teaching. Right away he singled me out, apparently thinking that if he could control me, he'd be able to control the rest of the gang. I was irritated and even more so when he dropped by the soda fountain where I was working to try to butter me up. I had started the summer out intending to behave myself—I'd been in enough trouble already and wanted to choose my battles—but this teacher was making it hard for me.

Things came to a head one day when I pulled a comic book out of the desk in front of me. Along with the book came a whole mess of crumpled papers and chewing-gum wrappers, which spilled under that desk and mine. The teacher decided to make a public illustration of me again: he stopped the class, embarrassed me in front of everyone and insisted that I pick up all the trash. I refused.

After class I decided to go see the teacher in his office and have a little talk with him. I was thoroughly rude and abusive. He was quite a bit shorter than me, and I grabbed him by the lapels and held him against the wall while I threatened his very existence if he didn't back off. Somehow I survived that class, but my friends continued to hound him to the point where he gave up teaching and became a sewing machine salesman.

My destructive anger didn't go away after I became a Christian. Learning to manage anger has been a lifelong struggle.

In the first year of our marriage, Shelby and I communicated well unless we had a problem. Whenever there was any tension—and it happened fairly often—Shelby would clam up. Her family had taught her that negative feelings were bad and the best thing to do was bury them. I found myself trying to argue both sides of the disagreement, which was frustrating at best.

One time I got incredibly angry and frustrated because Shelby would not respond to me. I didn't know what she was feeling or thinking, and I couldn't get her to tell me. I grabbed her by the shoulders and shook her, finally throwing her down on the bed. In horror, I watched as her head hit the wall, breaking a hole through the lath and plaster. I was shocked and panicked. The last thing I wanted to do was to hurt Shelby (and fortunately she wasn't seriously hurt, though she could easily have been). That experience shook me to the core. I had to find a better way to deal with my strong emotions.

I never physically abused Shelby again, but it was years before I felt I had gotten a handle on how to control my anger. I hated the destructive consequences of my anger. I hated myself at times, and found it hard to forgive myself, even if the person I had erupted on forgave me. People around me became aware of my angry outbursts and learned to walk gingerly for fear of provoking a tongue-lashing.

For example, one rainy day in Papua New Guinea I was on my way to the school, riding my motorcycle down the hill from our house. Halfway down the hill, the cycle slipped out from under me, and I went down on my hands and knees. I was going slow, so I didn't get too muddy. I continued on to school and began my usual routine. Putting my thermos of coffee down in my office, I went to turn on the bell system.

Nothing happened. The fuses had disappeared. Then I remembered it was April Fools' Day—the students must have "misplaced" the fuses. I hunted around and eventually found them. As soon as I got the fuses in, alarms and bells of every kind began to sound. The circuit board had been rewired. I'm not an electrician, but I found the extra wire and rang the bell.

I went back to my office to go over my talk for chapel that day. By this time I was ready for that coffee. I took a big gulp and just about spit it all over my desk. Another prankster had laced my thermos with salt!

When I walked into chapel, the students were nervous. They knew all about my angry tongue and were probably wondering if they'd crossed a line by messing with my coffee. Fortunately, I remembered the fun I'd had with practical jokes myself as a kid, and we enjoyed a good laugh over my adventures of the morning. It was good for them to see I wasn't angry.

Unfortunately, some of the other challenges I faced at Ukarumpa were not as happily resolved. As headmaster I prided myself on having an open-door policy. I placed an emphasis on trust and wanted teachers and parents to feel that I was approachable. At the same time, I was a workaholic and a driven person, probably conveying the sense that I was a little too busy to spend time on trivialities.

One day I walked into my office and noticed someone had left something on my desk. It was a petition signed by almost half of my faculty. At the head of the list was a senior teacher from Australia. The petition accused me—falsely—of a breach of professional ethics for criticizing a teacher in front of a student.

I was crushed. I felt hurt and betrayed; so many of the signatures were of friends of mine. I thought I had fostered a sense of trust and openness, but apparently the teachers didn't feel they could come to me and talk about their problem. What about my open door? What barriers did they see?

Finally I was angry—furious at the impersonal way they had communicated with me. I lashed out with accusations of my own. When we began to untangle what exactly had happened, it turned out that a student had overheard a portion of a conversation, which she misunderstood and added to before reporting it to her mother, who was a part-time teacher. The story was passed to a friend on the board, who talked to the Australian teacher. From his cultural context the way to deal with such a complaint was through a formal petition, so he began to gather signatures. It was weeks before it was settled.

Eventually I was exonerated, and it proved to be an opportunity for growth for me and for my team. I began to understand that a petition was a perfectly acceptable way for an Australian teacher to deal with a complaint against the headmaster. He expected me to respond in a similarly professional manner. My response arose out of all my insecurities.

Suddenly I wondered if everything I thought I was doing right was wrong. But because I was determined that we were there for the duration—after all we weren't going to desert the students—we had to find a way to understand each other. We began to discuss how Scripture applied to our working relationships. Some of the teachers argued that they were teachers who happened to be Christians, but I felt that we were Christians first and our relationships should be different from those of any secular teacher and principal. I wanted us to base our relationships on Scripture and use Matthew 18 as a guide to resolving conflict: go to the person who offended you first, then take a witness, and only then, if the person is still not receptive or repentant, present the situation to the church or larger community. It was a painful way to learn a lesson, but that principle of dealing with conflict on the level of resolving relationships between people has become a cornerstone to my whole philosophy of ministry and family life.

Part of my difficulty with anger arose from the way I was raised to believe that emotions were to be controlled. It was considered wrong and sinful to let emotions get the better of you, and I knew my explosions of anger were wrong. On the other hand, I didn't have a model for understanding what emotions are and how to manage them appropriately.

It was twenty years into our marriage, when Shelby and I decided to attend a Marriage Encounter weekend, that I began to understand the nature of emotions. They taught that emotions are not good or bad; they just are. We can respond to our emotions constructively or destructively, but the worst thing to do is pretend they aren't there. Emotions are energy, and if we don't express that energy, it finds ways of expressing itself—through physical symptoms like ulcers or psychological ones like depression. When we try to put a lid on anger, the pressure builds up until we explode—as happened so often to me—or it leaks out the sides and expresses itself in unintentional biting comments and sarcasm. Shelby and I learned to talk about our feelings, and a lot of that destructive force went out of my anger.

Another helpful lesson came from a psychologist who was a consultant in one of the ministries I worked in. He helped me become aware of the fact that I was always using euphemisms to talk about my anger. I would say that I was frustrated or upset, when really I was terribly angry. Naming my emotions is now another way for me to acknowledge and deal with them in positive ways. I have been much healthier since I learned to tell someone that I am angry because of a particular thing they said or did. Talking about anger in this way helps us to understand each other —often he or she had no intention of hurting me and no idea that I would take their statement that way. Sometimes I just misunderstood what they were saying. Open communication about feelings is part of reconciling relationships.

The Lord has built on that foundational principle by showing me another key to dealing with anger—namely, learning to tap into the power of forgiveness.

During our first furlough, some friends persuaded us to attend a Basic Youth Conflicts Seminar. It was the tail end of our first furlough year, and we were exhausted. We had come back from the field tired and a bit worn out, needing to find some nurture and rest, only to plunge into graduate studies, support raising and a serious health crisis for one of our daughters. We were so tired it was hard to pay attention, and my response to the conference was not entirely positive. But one very simple biblical principle gripped my heart that weekend: the importance of forgiveness. Bill Gothard emphasized the fact that Jesus died to see people reconciled—to God and to one another. It was the Christian's responsibility to at least attempt to keep all relationships reconciled. It had nothing to do with who hit whom. Broken relationships are destructive to all parties involved.

I was reminded that if I had an offense against a brother or sister, it would make my prayers ineffective. If I had an offense against a neighbor, the Lord really didn't want to receive my offerings. I didn't know whether that applied to the offering of my service. Years before Shelby and I had given ourselves to the Lord, dedicated each child to the Lord as she came along and given our lives to serving the Lord. Perhaps our service was unacceptable; I knew there were people I hadn't forgiven, and at the top of my list were my brothers and my sister and some of their spouses.

I didn't want to do it at all. I had been offended by my brothers and sister; I felt they were responsible to make it right with me. I argued with God. I thought up lots of reasons why I shouldn't have to do it. But I knew I must and began to take steps to meet with each of them. Each situation was extremely painful for me. I found it incredibly difficult to be obedient to God. In the process the Lord brought to my mind some things for which I was definitely responsible, where my attitudes and words and gossip had been wrong.

I had to forgive them too. As an act of the will I decided to forgive in advance, whether or not they would be willing to forgive me. I did talk to my siblings, and in each case there were tears and hugs, acceptance and forgiveness. It was an incredibly healing experience and the beginning of a new way of dealing with the angry vestiges of my dysfunctional past.

In 1975 our family witnessed a powerful demonstration of the healing potential of forgiving. We were on furlough and living in California. I had flown to New York for a missions conference where I was to be the main speaker for five days in a church that had supported our ministry for a number of years. Just before the conference started I received a telephone call from Shelby.

"Honey, I am in the hospital, and the surgeon wants to take a large lump out of my breast immediately." I couldn't believe my ears. I had no idea she even had a lump. "I'm coming home," I said. "Don't let them cut anything until I arrive." Those were the days when radical mastectomies were the norm for such cases. I explained the situation to the pastor and missions chairperson of the church, and they graciously encouraged me to go.

As it turned out there were conflicting opinions about the surgery, and she was allowed to go home. Frightened and feeling rather helpless, she called our pastor, Kerney Frantsen, and asked him to pray for her and anoint her with oil. Kerney came over immediately. He said to her, "Shelby, is there anyone you have not forgiven?" She was taken aback. What business was it of his whether she had not forgiven someone? What does that have to do with praying for God's healing?

Despite her misgivings, she answered, "Yes, there is someone I have not forgiven." It was a pastor who had been almost like a father to Shelby all during her teen-age years. Shelby was the first missionary from her home church, but while we were in Papua New Guinea, for reasons we did not understand, the pastor had stopped the church from supporting us and had told individuals in his congregation to do so as well. Shelby resented the pastor for this sudden withdrawal of support. It wasn't something she dwelt on, but it was there.

Kerney asked, "Are you willing to forgive him or her?" Shelby said, "Not really." "Well are you willing to ask the Lord to make you willing?" Shelby agreed to that and we all prayed together. Kerney prayed a beautiful prayer for her.

I still remember one of the things he said that day: "When you don't forgive someone, in some way that person is in jail, and you are the warden. You're incarcerated, too, because you have to make sure that the prisoner stays there."

Within two days of that prayer, Shelby got a telephone call from the wife of that pastor. She called to say that they had been praying for us, and they wanted us to know that they were going to start supporting us again. Shelby found herself willing to forgive the pastor—and did. A few days later the lump in her breast had disappeared.

Not long ago one of my colleagues in ministry erupted in the middle of a meeting, accused me of all sorts of things, and said that he'd been losing sleep over it. My immediate response was to be angry and hurt. I felt his outburst was out of proportion to reality, as well as being expressed in an inappropriate way in the middle of a meeting of our peers. Just as I was about to start explaining myself, the Lord helped me to see the experience from his perspective and feel some of what he was feeling. I recognized that I was in some way responsible for that hurt. I said to him, "I feel awful that you lost sleep over this. I want to ask your forgiveness for being insensitive to your feelings and not investing the time to explain what I was doing and why." It blew him away. A potentially divisive conflict within our ministry team was averted, and we were able to work out our problem peacefully.

Seeking forgiveness and reconciliation comes more easily to me today than it did almost twenty years ago when I first started practicing these principles. I have discovered that the consequences of forgiving are out of all proportion to the act of forgiving, as difficult as that act seems at times. It has been very important in my recovery to recognize my responsibility for alienation in relationships, the need to forgive and accept and seek reconciliation.

# 6

## *From Workaholism to Balance*

In 1948 my parents were ready to return to China. We had been living in Corning, New York, and our journey back to Asia would involve driving to the West Coast, camping along the way to save money and sailing from San Francisco.

Frank was eleven and a member of a winning Little League team. The day we were supposed to leave Corning was the day of the state championship. Frank was a key player on his team, and I still remember the pain and disappointment we felt at having to miss that game, along with any national games the team might have qualified for. It was a bitter reminder to us kids that our parent's ministry always came first—and especially so because we missed the ship when my mother became ill for a short time. We never did go back to China. In the weeks we waited for another ship, relations between the United States and China broke down, and we lost our visas.

All through my youth, I resented the fact that my parents took seriously the command to "seek first the kingdom of God and his righteousness" (Mt 6:33). They weren't intentionally neglecting our needs; they sincerely believed that God would take care of their children. But I didn't like it, and I resolved that things would be different in my home. I came to believe that seeking the kingdom of God meant I couldn't neglect my responsibility to my family. I was convinced that my children could be a positive part of my ministry, not mere appendages that got dragged from place to place against their will. I had no idea how difficult it would be for me, especially because I decided to teach missionary children overseas.

I'm sure that part of my attraction to the role of teaching missionary kids arose from my own background. I could identify with their experiences, the feeling that they were "different." They never quite belonged either to American culture or to the culture of the people their parents served. I wanted them to feel good about their differences in ways that I hadn't felt good about myself. I wanted to encourage missionary families to find a healthy balance between meeting the needs of their children and pursuing the ministry that God had called them to. In the early years in Papua New Guinea I remember thinking that if I could keep one missionary couple on the field for one year without having to worry about how their kids were doing, I would have accomplished something truly worthwhile for the kingdom. Looking back, I'm sure I did that many times over.

I set up a system where the school and the teachers formed the backbone of the socialization process for the children, but their first responsibility was to help the kids honor their parents and appreciate their ministry. There was enough flexibility so that younger children could go back and forth fairly frequently between the school and the village where their parents were. The teachers had to enable the parents to teach the kids at home during those times, and would even get on the ham radio once a week to update the child on daily events in the classroom, so they didn't feel they had missed anything. If a parent was having trouble, say with teaching fractions, the teacher could say, "Don't worry, we'll cover that next week." Everything was designed so that the children could enjoy the nurture of their parents and the educational advantages of the school, and come to appreciate the culture their parents were working in.

Meanwhile, I was too busy to spend much time with my own family. I was a full-time teacher. I was the only guidance counselor. I was the principal. I was an anthropology consultant, teaching seminars and assisting translators in various ways. I was conducting anthropological research in the tribal areas on school holidays. I was a workaholic, a driven person. I was determined to succeed, and because I felt insecure, I thought I had to work harder than anyone else. I was determined to do everything and do it right. I was killing myself in order to give other missionary families some of the things I had missed growing up, and for the longest time, I was blind to the fact that I was denying them to my own family. God had to slow me down.

Toward the end of the first term in Papua New Guinea I was struck with the most severe case of mononucleosis that our mission doctor had ever seen. I was panic-stricken. The doctor ordered a month's bed rest. I had seen some of my colleagues battle the chronic consequences of the virus for six months or a year or longer. *Oh God,* I pleaded, *please don't let this happen.* What would happen to the school? What about all these things I was involved in?

I called one of the teachers. "John, would you gather four other teachers and come to my house and anoint me with oil and pray for my healing?" Little did I know that none of the teachers invited had ever prayed for anyone's healing in this manner, according to the instructions in James 5:14-15. Several of them were scared to death, both because it was a new experience and because they were afraid of catching mono. God answered their prayer, and within twenty-four hours I felt completely better. I was a little weak, but all the symptoms were gone.

It was a school holiday, so I felt I could respond to Shelby's insistence that I take a few days off. I rested and spent some time reflecting on the past four years. There were many things I was grateful for, many things I'd been able to accomplish that I felt good about. I began to thank God for some of those opportunities, and with each one I mentioned, I had a strong impression that the Lord was saying to me, "That's not important." He wasn't too interested in my long hours and hard work, the seminars and trips and the people I'd touched. What he kept saying to me was, "My son, what about you? I am more interested in what I am doing in you than in what I am doing through you."

He was just a loving Father trying to get my attention and to let me know that he had seen some progress in my walk of faith. The things he wanted to affirm were the changes in me, things like learning what it meant to live and work in community and put other people's interests ahead of my own. It was a humbling experience because God didn't seem to care about accomplishments as much as I did. Yet it was thrilling because he showed how much he cares about me.

As a workaholic my identity hinged on my performance and accomplishments. I was the headmaster. If I felt I was doing a good job, and the school was functioning smoothly and students were learning, I could feel good about who I was. One of the crippling effects of my dysfunctional past is the tendency to find my self-esteem in things outside myself, rather than in the simple fact of God's love for me.

I've always loved my work and always loved being busy. I enjoyed the big challenges. For many years, my idea of a vacation was to pack up my briefcase with backlogged correspondence and drive Shelby and the kids to the beach. If Shelby actually insisted on my spending time with the kids making sand castles, I'd grumble and make sure she realized how much important work I was not getting done. The word *relax* wasn't in my vocabulary.

When we came home for our first furlough, our pace only increased. I had been asked to form an international children's education department for Wycliffe, and I decided I'd better get a teaching credential since I was beginning to set standards for teachers entering Wycliffe. As usual, I set myself to do the impossible: I wanted to finish my program in education in less than a year and become certified as a teacher and a principal. In addition, we had the normal furlough activities such as speaking in churches, visiting family and friends, and fundraising. We were living in New Jersey where we had free missionary housing and the schools were more affordable, but we missed the nurture and support of our home church in Ithaca.

One night in January we were coming home after a weekend of meetings. As she was walking to bed, two-year-old Tonya, normally a very sure-footed child, stumbled. I was puzzled but then noticed that she was dragging her foot.

The next morning we took her to the doctor, who immediately admitted her to the hospital. She was there for ten days, with Shelby and I each taking twelve-hour shifts to stay with her around the clock. The doctors couldn't figure out what was causing the loss of feeling Tonya was experiencing. One night Shelby prayed that the doctors would see something they hadn't seen before. The next morning they came and nearly went without seeing anything new. Shelby, who had been watching Tonya carefully, said, "Did you notice that Tonya is now having difficulty raising her arm?"

The doctor blanched. He was frightened. After confirming her observation, he took Shelby outside the room and said, "This is very serious. You and the baby must be transferred immediately to Philadelphia Children's Hospital."

Shelby was scared to death. She couldn't reach me by phone. She cried, pulled herself together, powdered her nose and went back into the room. She smiled as she picked Tonya up and held her, but Tonya looked at her and said, "Mama, why are you afraid?"

At Philadelphia Children's Hospital, team after team of doctors poked and pounded and did spinal taps and other diagnostic procedures before determining that Tonya had a rare condition called Guillian-Beret Syndrome. There was no cure and no treatment. The condition causes paralysis to creep through the body, eventually hitting the vital organs. There was no way to reverse the paralysis, and we just had to pray that it would stop before it reached Tonya's vital organs.

I called four of our supporting churches and told them, "If you have ever prayed for us, do it now." I didn't have the faith to ask them to pray for complete healing. I simply asked them to pray that God would stop the paralysis before it reached her heart and lungs. Tonya got to the point where she was like a piece of cooked spaghetti. She had no muscle control, even in her mouth. But God answered our prayer that her heart and lungs wouldn't be affected. As we saw this answer to prayer, we began to ask people to pray that God would reverse the condition. He graciously responded and Tonya gradually got better. She was completely restored.

During the time Tonya was in the hospital I put aside most of the myriad of things I was doing. I had one priority, and that was being with my gravely ill daughter. But when there was no dramatic emergency, I was still having trouble putting limits on my work for the sake of my family.

It took one more complete breakdown of health in my family to get me to deal with my workaholism. This time it was Shelby. We came back from Papua New Guinea in 1974. I had decided that trying to run the school in Ukarumpa and serve as superintendent for all of Wycliffe's schools was too much. I asked my superiors which job they wanted me to do, and they said, "Come back to the United States and run the Children's Education Department."

Shelby had been having health problems for some time, and the doctors hadn't been able to get to the bottom of it. Yet she was determined to get a master's degree in special education in order to build on some of her experiences in Ukarumpa of helping kids with reading problems. Her symptoms were becoming more acute, and the stress of managing a home, caring for four children and her education were not helping.

We later learned that she had acute hypoglycemia. She would drink coffee and eat a candy bar and then go take an exam. After the exam she would get in the car and black out. Sometimes she would feel it coming on as she drove home on the freeway, pull off the road and faint.

I was concentrating on developing my job as superintendent and wasn't aware of what was happening to Shelby. My budget for travel was small, and when I heard about that chance to catch a free ride to Brazil with a friend of mine who was a missionary pilot, I jumped at the opportunity. There was no real reason for going, but I figured it would be good to visit and encourage the Wycliffe teachers there. I was gone for four weeks, and it was obvious that God was blessing that trip. I touched some lives, and saw God take care of us in amazing ways. But in a lot of ways, I had no business being there. I needed to be with Shelby; there was a real precariousness in her life. She could have had one of those fainting spells in the middle of traffic and been killed. Even worse, I had almost no contact with her the whole time I was gone. (I've since learned to call regularly when I travel.)

When I got back from Brazil, the seriousness of her situation started to sink in. I started to realize, as well, that the pressures she was living under were responsible for destroying her health. Some of those pressures had to do with being a woman missionary. People were always asking Shelby what she did, and telling them she was raising four young children never seemed adequate. That pressure was behind her determination to get her master's degree at a time when she should have been taking care of her health problems. And probably more than anything else, there were pressures from me, the destructive influences of my uncontrolled anger and critical tongue, that contributed to her ill health.

It was later that same year that I quickly flew home from a missions conference to be with Shelby when she thought she would have to have surgery. That was an important experience because I had to put my money where my mouth was. I always have opinions, and I've given a lot of advice over the years, but I don't always take my own advice. I didn't struggle with that decision; I knew what I had to do and did it, and fortunately my hosts were understanding. But I could see that I would have struggled over similar circumstances before that. At some level I think I understood that part of Shelby's illness was due to my behavior and upside-down priorities. That helped me to do the right thing.

Another way God has helped me become a more balanced person is through reaching out to other people who also struggle with workaholism. It's always a helpful way of reinforcing the principles he has taught me, and occasionally the rewards are surprising. One of those who helped me much more than I helped him was Jim Smotherman.

I met Jim when he was principal of the mission school at Yarinacocha, Peru, and I visited as superintendent. He was very highly esteemed by everyone—parents, students and the local community. I could see that he was working too hard, and I talked to him about learning how to say no and putting some boundaries on his involvements. I'm sure it must have sounded good, but he didn't know how to do it. He seemed like he had it all together in the spiritual and physical realms, with his family dynamics and in his relations with parents, teachers and kids. But he was just being used up, consumed. He got to the point where he would lie on his floor at ten o'clock at night dictating letters—he couldn't sit, stand or lie down except on the floor because of excruciating tension pain.

Finally, Jim came home on furlough. He'd say things like, "I think I'll go get a truck-driving job." He didn't want to ever see another missionary kid or missionary family. He would have been happy to stay away from Wycliffe completely. He didn't want any kind of responsibility, not even teaching Sunday school.

I kept looking for signs of progress, but it seemed he was going downhill. One day I was on my way over to visit him, and I just cried out to the Lord. I had no idea how to help him or what to say to him. The Lord impressed upon me the importance of inviting him to come and work for me. That seemed to me like a crazy idea. It did to Jim too. "Dan, I'm a cripple!" he argued. "I can't do anything for you."

I replied, "I can't help it. The Lord told me to say that to you, and I just have to believe it's right."

"I haven't got anything to offer. I'm burnt out," he responded. He was full of self-recrimination, frustrated with himself for not taking charge of his life and allowing these things to get to him. He expressed his anger against those who supervised him, although he did it in a typically gentle way.

Eventually he did come to work with me, and we set the terms together. I told him he had to have some absolute boundaries, and I was going to make sure he stuck to them. Much to my surprise his limits were even more strict than the ones I suggested. We had said he would work half-time, but he started out with two days a week. When the clock ticked five o'clock, he was out of there.

As I recall, for the first month, there was little or nothing that Jim was able to do or produce. We spent hours and hours together. I tried to share some of my dreams and vision, but sometimes that put pressure on him because he felt he ought to be helping. Much more of the time I spent listening to him, pulling out of him what happened to him, what it meant, how he was going to prevent it happening again, how was he going to get stronger. We trusted God for change. We talked about issues like forgiveness, healing and restoration, and I shared with him honestly how I struggled with some of those same issues.

I learned so much from him. I admired his strength in making those small but significant decisions. "I will not work more than twenty hours, period." And, more importantly, he held himself to that commitment. I'd never seen that in my life. He found ways of getting other people to help, and he got the job done.

When I left that position, I tried to get him to take my job. He was the most logical candidate. He absolutely refused, except to take it for a brief time in an acting capacity. He knew it was not for him. He never wanted to live like he had lived before, and he didn't care what title or prestige was offered to him. He wanted to be a healthy person; he wanted to live his commitments to God without sacrificing his own health or his relationship with his family. I learned from him that it was OK to set some absolute boundaries on my life. He was able to go home at night and just turn off the office. He taught himself not to allow the office to dominate his thinking. His example still challenges me.

I have now learned how to take a vacation without dragging my briefcase along. The first time this happened was shortly after we moved back to the United States. Before leaving town, I told my secretary that I would check in with her every other day. Four or five days into the vacation, Shelby said, "Weren't you going to call your secretary?" I had completely forgotten the office, my secretary, even the fact I had a secretary. We have had some wonderful vacations since I learned that I'm not indispensible and that people can manage without me for a week or two.

Over the years I have tried to pay more attention to the principle of the Sabbath too. For people in ministry, Sunday is rarely a day of rest. Many of my weekends are spent preaching or teaching, yet I'm still not consistent in setting aside another day of the week for that time of rest and recreation. God established the seventh day as a day of rest for a good reason—he knew human beings need times of quiet and rest, time to be refreshed and refilled by spending time in God's presence. I love being busy, having too much to do, having many options and activities to choose from. The Sabbath reminds me that even though I thrive on activity and a frantic pace, that busyness I love can be a killer.

One area I still have to work hard at is travel. Sometimes I have to make tough decisions to limit my travel. At other times, I've taken Shelby or one of the girls with me on trips. I've learned some ways to keep my family involved in my ministry even when I'm away and to balance my responsibility to them with the opportunities of ministry. I make it a point to call home every day if I'm in the country, and at least once a week from overseas. It's expensive, but communicating with my family is important. When I get back from a long trip, I don't go into the office for the first few days. I don't even unpack my briefcase. I listen to Shelby and my daughters. I catch up on what they've been doing. When the girls were younger, I made it a point not to re-enter the children's discipline pattern for a couple of days. My wick is short at those times and it's better if I don't disrupt the dynamic Shelby has had with the girls.

A concept that helps me deal with my tendency toward workaholism is *equipoise*, the balancing of roles. I play a number of different roles in life; each one has its own responsibilities and expectations: husband, father, supervisor, employee, church member, board member, just to name a few. My goal is to keep these roles in balance so that no single role is emphasized to the detriment of the others. It also means that I have to give up my perfectionism: I can't be the perfect father and the perfect husband and the perfect employee all at the same time. Some things are worth doing but not worth doing perfectly.

I don't always manage to keep my balance. For example, my daughter Melody went through my calendar for 1989 and counted up that I was away from the office 244 days that year, mostly on trips. That goes against everything I believe in, and I wouldn't have been aware of the problem if Melody hadn't taken the time to analyze my calendar. I'm starting out 1990 determined to do it differently.

# 7

# *From Guilt to Acceptance*

hen we lived in Papua New Guinea, Karl and Joice
Franklin, the couple who had gotten us involved in
Wycliffe at Cornell, remained our close friends.
They were translators working among the Kewa,
a people still living in a Stone Age culture in the remote southern highlands. During school breaks our family would visit the Franklins in the village where they lived. I would work on anthropology research projects while Shelby helped out in other ways.

When the Franklins first went into the area, they decided to take as few things as possible from the outside world, but once they determined they could stay there long-term and learn and codify the language, they brought in five 44-gallon drums. They had organized their supplies so they would open up only one drum at a time. The Kewa people have very few possessions, so the whole region speculated eagerly about what was in those other drums. Finally, one of the leaders in the village came to Karl and announced, "We figured it out. We figured out what you have in those other barrels."

"What?" Karl asked.

He responded, "Your other four wives."

One day I found out there was a plane taking supplies to the Franklins. I rushed home to ask Shelby if she had anything we could send them, like baked goods or fresh vegetables. Shelby didn't think she had anything to send. "What about that head of lettuce in the fridge?" I asked.

"Dan, you know we're having guests tonight," she answered. "I was planning to make a salad for them. It's been a long time since we had a head of lettuce. Please don't ask me to send that to the Franklins."

"You can get the special things that come into our commissary; the Franklins can't," I replied. I went on and on until she finally gave in and handed me the lettuce to take to the airstrip.

I went back to school and ended up working later than I planned. (I was supposed to help her get ready for the evening.) As I was rushing home, the parent of one of my students stopped me along the road. He wanted to talk about his daughter and the school. Just as I was starting to feel fidgety because I knew I should be home helping Shelby, he said, "Oh, could you use some lettuce?" He went over to his garden and plucked two fresh heads and gave them to me. God had provided for our guests as well as the Franklins!

Shelby is a generous person who responds to needs with all her resources. But by insisting we send that head of lettuce I put her in a real bind: Should she be generous to our dinner guests or to the Franklins? I put a guilt trip on her so that she would do what I wanted. It wasn't fair to her, yet she responded graciously.

This kind of manipulation, putting pressure on someone to do what I wanted, comes right out of my own insecurity. I was worried that the Franklins would think badly of us because we didn't send them something special. In reality, the thought would probably never have crossed their minds, but I needed people to think well of me.

One of my favorite cartoons is a Ziggy cartoon on the "Ought to Syndrome." The first panel shows Ziggy walking up to his mailbox. "I ought to clean the bird's nest out of here," he says. In the next panel, he's walking into his house. "I ought to fix that crack in the ceiling." The last panel is Ziggy saying, "I ought to stop oughting myself."

As a teacher and headmaster of the school, I often felt my work was never done. I ought to be grading papers, ought to be spending time with my family, ought to be spending more time with the teachers, ought to be learning more about the curricula and history of the fifteen countries represented by the students in my school.

And because I was consumed with the "I oughts" in my own life, it was easy for me to say "you ought" to other people. One person who came under the pressure of my false guilt trips was Glandion Carney, a pastor who went with me on a mission trip to Taiwan and the Philippines in 1981. It was his first international crosscultural experience, and I was excited about the prospect of getting him into a village in the Philippines where he could experience tribal ministry firsthand.

Glandion was nervous. As we approached the trip to the village, he was being bombarded with stories that made him more and more fearful. We spent time with various missionaries along the way, including my brother Bob and his wife. Missionaries are fond of telling their horror stories of snakes, accidents and other dangers. I've heard dozens, perhaps hundreds, of snake stories, but I never once saw a snake in the nine years we lived in Papua New Guinea. News reports of a horrible bus accident in the Philippines were giving Glandion nightmares.

The last straw came when I told Glandion that I would not be going with him to the village. I had business in Manila, and there was only so much space in the helicopter that would be taking him and two missionary women into the village. Now Glandion was really scared.

The night before the trip, he woke me in the middle of the night. "Dan, I'm not going," he said. I was half asleep and certainly not in a frame of mind to listen to his fears. I started in on him. I reminded him that it had cost a lot of money to get him to the Philippines. A lot of people were praying that he would have an in-depth experience with some Bible translators. I told him he wouldn't have as many stories to tell back at his church if he didn't go. I said some more manipulative things and went back to sleep.

Despite my less than compassionate response Glandion sorted things out with the Lord and decided to face his fears and go ahead. The tribe we had arranged for him to visit was the Negreto people, a tribe of black-skinned pygmies. They were very impressed with Glandion: not only was he black, he was a giant compared to them. God used Glandion to minister to them, and the experience touched his heart and opened his eyes to the worldwide mission of the church.

A day or two later, Glandion had the opportunity to share the story at the Wycliffe center there in the Philippines. He told about my "encouraging" words; I was a little embarrassed. But he had decided to go, not because I put pressure on him but because he felt the Lord wanted him there and he would trust the Lord. I realized I had been selfish in what I said to him. I was more concerned that my colleagues and the donor who sponsored Glandion's trip would think I had wasted their money than I was about Glandion. I had to ask him to forgive me.

Guilt is a powerful human emotion. It is God's way of letting us know we've wandered off the path. But we can also experience a false sense of guilt that comes from other people trying to manipulate us or simply from the evil one, who is the accuser. I struggled with guilt and false guilt from childhood, and learning to tell the difference has been an important part of my growth.

When I was nine years old I got my first pair of glasses. At the time, my Dad asked what must have been a perfectly natural question, Why had my eyes deteriorated? The optometrist said, "It's because the boy reads too much." As a child, I had loved to read. I used to go to bed at night and read with a flashlight under the covers. Well, when I heard the optometrist blame my reading habits for my poor eyesight, I believed him. I didn't read another book until I had to, which was in college. Of course, I later learned that most children who require glasses for shortsightedness get them around age nine. It had nothing to do with reading, but I felt guilty for destroying my eyesight all the same.

I experienced real guilt as a child too. I feared going to hell.

My parents had drilled into me the truths of the Christian faith from my earliest days. I had to memorize Bible verses before leaving the house and repeat them back when I got home. I never doubted that what they taught me was the truth, but I was not willing to repent and accept that truth. During my teen years I recall many times when I would come home and nobody would be there. My parents were usually out at a Child Evangelism class or some other church activity, but they never left a note telling me when they would return. I would imagine that the rapture had taken place, and I was left behind. I knew that I was going to hell, and the fear and power of those thoughts would almost overwhelm me. By the time my parents returned I would be frantic, but I didn't dare tell them what I had been thinking and feeling. I knew what their response would be, and I didn't want to be told that my fears were justified and that I should repent.

Those guilty feelings were frightening things, to be hidden and denied. My understanding of God was that he was some sort of bad guy, a boogieman to be feared, not a loving, gracious person. After I became a Christian, my picture of God began to change. I experienced his love and forgiveness, and gradually, I understood that he had limitless grace and forgiveness to deal with all the guilt I felt. "If we confess our sins, he is faithful and just and will forgive us our sins and purify us from all unrighteousness" (1 Jn 1:9).

If we don't confess our guilt to God and ask his forgiveness, the consequences of that guilt are inevitably destructive. King David is a good example of this. When he committed adultery with Bathsheba and she became pregnant, David didn't face up to his guilt but instead tried to cover his tracks. He manipulated her husband, Uriah, to try to get him to sleep with her so he would think the child was his. When that didn't work, David arranged for Uriah to be killed. The suffering didn't end there, however. The child died, and later a good deal more misery came upon David's family as well.

But that isn't the end of the story for David. He was confronted with his sin by the prophet Nathan, and he did repent and acknowledge his sin. He trusted God to forgive him, and God restored him. He is known as a man after God's heart, and he's on the honor roll of God's favorite people of faith in Hebrews 11. David sinned—spectacularly—but his repentance was genuine.

Sometimes it's hard to tell the difference between real guilt, which is God's way of getting us to turn back to him, and false guilt, which is the enemy's accusation telling us we're not good enough for God's love. When I was in graduate school in Dallas, Shelby and I had a small group of friends who would get together every Monday night to talk and debate, sometimes until the wee hours of the morning. I learned much more from them than I did from any of my formal classes. We became very close friends, and we realized that the others represented enormous potential for the kingdom. We pushed and stretched and encouraged and affirmed and challenged one another.

Marshall was one of the members of the group. He came from a very rigid fundamentalist background, and quite frankly he took a beating in our group. To some extent we all had similar backgrounds, but I felt I had been freed from some of the rigid legalism that we had all grown up around. I wanted Marshall to experience some of that freedom, too, but in many ways I was flaunting my freedom at his expense. Misapplying my freedom, I thought that if it didn't bother me to have a glass of wine on occasion, it shouldn't bother him. Well, it did.

We left for Papua New Guinea in July 1966. The following year Marshall transferred from Dallas Seminary to Perkins. Later, he left the church and ministry. He had what amounted to a mental breakdown. His psychiatrist told him that all he needed to do to get well was to throw out his religion; it was his rigid fundamentalism that was destroying him. Marshall believed him.

We kept in touch with Marshall from the field, and it was deeply distressing to me to hear what he was going through. At times I even wondered if I should make a special trip home to try to help him. I felt guilty about Marshall's rejection of his faith, yet I didn't really want to think about it. The news we heard about Marshall kept getting worse: he had become an alcoholic; during Ph.D. studies in Holland his marriage was falling apart.

A number of years later, I got a letter from him, in which he said, "I know you may feel guilty about certain things, but I don't want you to feel guilty." My first reaction was defensiveness—I don't feel guilty! But when I let myself think about it, I had to admit that I did. That is when I had to acknowledge my guilt: I had not respected the needs of a brother. But I was carrying a load of guilt for some things that were not my responsibility. I had no control over whether Marshall would reject Christ or not; I wasn't responsible for his drinking or the breakup of his marriage.

Seventeen years later, I received a telephone message from Marshall. It simply said, "God wants it all and has restored the peace after so many years." Marshall had returned to the Lord.

As my children have grown into adulthood, I have had to work very hard against my tendency to impose my expectations on others through guilt or manipulation. Not too long ago I came across a Bible study guide based on the Twelve Steps. I thought it might be useful for us to work through the program as a family, and I asked Paula if she would be willing to coordinate the program for us. She has developed an ability to help two members of our family who are having a conflict to hear one another and settle their differences through understanding. I thought she would be able to give valuable leadership as we went through this Twelve Steps program. Paula considered my request carefully and decided she didn't have time to take on another commitment.

I was reassured when she came and said no, because I know my daughters want to please me—they don't say no to me very often. Of course, any father is delighted when his children do something to please him, but I don't want them to please me out of fear or a sense of coercion. I want them to be their own persons and act out of their own sense of what is right or what is best. Realizing that my children feel free to make their own choices encourages me to believe that my dysfunctional pattern of false guilt hasn't been passed on to them.

# 8

# *Honor Thy Father and Mother*

W̲e must make sure that every new Wycliffe recruit hears your testimony!" I had just shared my story with a group of new missionaries-in-training with Wycliffe, and I was surprised to see Dr. Kenneth Pike and his wife, Evelyn, both early leaders in Wycliffe, come up to me with such enthusiastic reactions. "Your parents must have done something right," added Dr. Pike.

I was terribly uncomfortable. I wasn't sure that I had given my parents credit for doing anything right. I wondered if I should ever share my story again if I couldn't do it in a way that gave my parents the respect they deserved. I wanted to encourage others who had rocky starts in life, but as I mulled over that experience, I became convinced that I had to take seriously God's command to honor my father and mother.

While I recognize the significant problems in my parent's home and the lasting effects in my life, coming to terms with that past and learning to respect my parents has been a key part of the healing God has done in my life. Very soon after I became a Christian, it became clear to me that I had to reconcile with my father. I decided to forgive him—as a simple act of the will, not because he asked me to or because I felt any differently. That was the beginning of a new relationship with him, one that had its ups and downs certainly, but a relationship based on respect.

As I already shared, God used the three years I spent with my parents while I attended Cornell to help me see my parents in a new light. Mark Twain once wrote that he was amazed at how wise his parents had become in the course of several years when he was away from them. Something like that happened to my parents too. They didn't change, but God had changed my attitude toward them. I learned to appreciate things that had offended me terribly as a child. I learned about my parents' own pains.

Beatrice Shippey and Stanley Harrison sailed for China in 1921. They had been courting for some time, but the mission would not allow them to marry until they had learned the Tibetan language. After two years of language study they married and settled in the village of Hetsuohen among Tibetans.

My sister Beth was born a year later, and Bruce came two years later. My mother had been a high school teacher and principal, so she taught Beth and Bruce until they were eleven and nine. Then my parents felt it was in their best interest to put them in boarding school. My Dad took them on a five-day trip by horseback, and then on by truck and to the mission school in central China. When they finished what schooling was available there, some furloughing missionaries brought them to another school in Viet Nam. Between the time they left for school and when they reached adulthood, they probably spent a few months with our parents. When they wrote a letter home, it took three months to get there. If they shared a problem, it took six months to get an answer. In the end, they stopped sharing problems.

Bruce and Beth went off to school years before I was born. My mother told me this story and her understanding of its meaning. To me it epitomized the destructive consequences of parental commitments to "seek first the Kingdom of God." My parents were not very demonstrative, and they believed they should be "strong" in front of the children, not letting on that this separation hurt them deeply. I think Bruce and Beth interpreted that strength as lack of feeling, as if they didn't care that their children were away for years at a time. It was only in talking about it with them years later that I learned that my parents were devastated by the separation. They would leave the room and weep, they missed their kids so much. How sad that they never let them know it.

Years later when we were in Papua New Guinea, I received a letter from my mother. She wrote, "I'm going to Bruce and Kay's. They have invited me to come and stay for a long time, perhaps as long as eighteen months or two years. Bruce wants to get to know me." At that time, Bruce was over fifty years old, pastoring a Baptist church.

Later, I received another letter from my mother that was mailed from a different part of the country. She made no mention of Bruce and Kay. I thought I knew what had happened, and I was outraged at the idea that Bruce had rejected his own mother. Later, Bruce told me that every time he sat across the table from "that wrinkled old woman" who was a stranger to him, the feelings of loneliness, resentment and desertion welled up within him. He had wanted to get to know his mother, but the price was just too high. I realized I had been wrong to judge Bruce. There was no way I could ever understand what he had suffered in those years of separation. The incident made me all the more grateful for those years I had with my parents and the opportunity to be reconciled to them.

And the more I heard about their ministry among Tibetans, the more I admired them for their faithfulness in bearing fruit for God. Two years after they settled in Hetsuohen, a young hereditary chieftain named Wan De Ker became a believer. He had a strong testimony and readily shared it. He and my father would go into the marketplace, where my father would play the trumpet to get people's attention. Then Wan De Ker would give his testimony and my father would preach. Many people became interested, including some of the Buddhist priests. This frightened the Buddhist leaders in the community, and within two weeks after his conversion, Wan De Ker was murdered by his neighbors. His mouth was stuffed with stones, and his body was dragged by the feet through the streets of Hetsuohen behind a horse. This tragic experience would have been enough to cause most people to quit, but my folks were just beginning.

The mission leaders suggested that my parents move to a different location. They considered that advice, but Mom and Dad felt that God had called them there and they should stay. The response was slow. They taught Bible classes and some

Tibetans became secret Christians. When they left China after more than twenty years, only a handful of converts were willing to be identified as Christians.

My parents were always pioneers, even mavericks. On one occasion, my Dad was traveling in a remote area with a Tibetan helper. They were lost in the fog on a dark night in treacherous mountain terrain. Then they heard dogs barking from an encampment somewhere up ahead. The helper was so fearful that he was unable to provide assistance. My Dad took over. He shouted out in Tibetan to the head of the encampment, who responded to his call and navigated the two strangers into the camp by shouting instructions to them. It was like someone in a control tower telling a passenger how to land a plane.

Only in the light of the next morning did the head of the encampment realize that he had been talking to a "foreign devil." He never would have helped my father if he had known that, but my father's grasp of the language and culture was so good he could pass for a Tibetan—at least in the dark.

My Dad did a lot of unconventional things to win the trust of the people he was ministering to. Missionaries were encouraged in those days to pay more than the buyer asked, as a demonstration of generosity. My father quickly discovered that the Tibetans considered paying more a demonstration of stupidity. He always bought low and sold high, and became highly respected as an astute trader. He learned the Tibetan system of barter, which involved putting your hand inside the other man's long sheepskin sleeve and negotiating by tapping on his hand.

My parents were medical missionaries, not because they were formally trained but because people came to them in need of help. One day people from a nearby village came running to get *Aka Shedub Jemsin* (the transliteration of Dr. Stanley Harrison). A woman had fallen off a roof and hit her head, splitting it open from the eyebrow to the back of her neck. My father protested there was nothing he could do for such an injury, but they insisted that he come and perform a miracle.

The first thing Dad did was to pray for the woman. Then he cleaned her off as best he could, gently pressed her brain back into its cavity, sutured her up and hoped for the best. Some time later he returned to that village, and there was the same woman, with a smile on her face, feeling eternally indebted to the great foreign "doctor."

During his furloughs, my father talked his way into understudying specialists who could help him serve the people more effectively. He learned the rudiments of surgery, the treatment of venereal diseases and agriculture. They introduced new strains of barley and potatoes that were hardy enough to thrive at altitudes above 10,000 feet. At a time when the mission authorities were convinced that the existing Tibetan Bible was sufficient (it was translated into a very formal dialect known only to a minority of the priests), my father burned the midnight oil to put God's Word into the language of the people.

Even though we left China when I was only three, I was privileged to share in one of the greatest thrills of my parents' ministry. They received a letter in 1961 from a Swedish missionary who was working among Tibetan refugees in India. This missionary had gone to great lengths to find *Aka Shedub Jemsin,* about whom the refugees from Amdo/Gansu province continually talked. They spoke of Dad as the person who had set a broken leg, pulled a tooth, cured them of venereal disease, fixed a clock and always spoke of the Jesus person.

This letter included a long list of the Tibetans who had become Christians in India. When the Swedish missionary began to explore the planting of the seed he was privileged to reap, he discovered that behind it was the faithful witness of Beatrice and Stanley Harrison. Some people might have left that little handful of believers in Tibet, thinking that twenty-three years of ministry had been a failure. My parents never did; they believed their responsibility was to be faithful, not to see success in terms of numbers.

About five years ago, a friend of ours wrote us from Gansu province, where he was teaching English. He told us that a number of his students were from Hetsuohen, and they had reported that the church there is doing well, with a substantial number of Tibetans in it. Around Hetsuohen there are perhaps as many as 10,000 believers, many of them Tibetans. The seeds planted by my parents and other faithful people like them continue to bear fruit to this day.

Many values that my parents held strongly have now borne fruit in my own life. Even as a rebellious teen, some of their values had sunk in to me and kept me from certain disaster. One day my friends and I ditched school and hitchhiked from Ithaca to Cortland, twenty-three miles away. I bought a large jug of wine and we all got drunk. Toward the afternoon someone suggested we should steal a car and go home. I refused to have anything to do with it; that was a line I just wouldn't cross. I don't remember how I got home that day, but it wasn't in a stolen car.

My parents taught me that God is powerful and that he answers prayer. Even after years of rebellion and rejecting God I didn't find this hard to believe once I gave my life to Christ.

I knew my parents prayed for me. When they died, I felt like a spiritual rug had been pulled out from under me. I wondered if I would ever be able to do anything useful again without their undergirding prayers.

They believed that the door to China would reopen for ministers of the gospel, and they prayed faithfully for the believers and the growth of the church there. They had their bags packed virtually until the day they died, expecting to return there themselves. The door did open, and I believe it had a lot to do with their prayers and the prayers of others like them. I had the privilege of serving for two years with English Language Institute/China, one of the organizations that is sending Christians into China to teach English to university students. My daughter Paula taught there for a year as well.

My parents never described people by their differences; they really were colorblind. My best friend in high school was Paul Whitted. Paul's father was half-black and half-white, and his mother was half-American Indian and half-white. My parents loved Paul and were happy that he was my best friend. It was quite a while before I learned that his parents were not accepted by either of their families or by the community around them.

This was another value that bore fruit in my difficult teen years —the street gang I led was the only multi-ethnic gang in town, and in various ways I tried to act as a peacemaker in the turf wars of other gangs.

My parents stood up for their beliefs even when it wasn't the popular thing to do. The church that had sent them to the mission field was in a neighborhood that was changing economically and ethnically during my teen years. People of color were moving in, and some were starting to attend the church services. The church was very mission-minded and contributed a high percentage to missions, but the elders in quiet ways would let these newcomers know that they were not welcome. This subtle racism infuriated my father, and he stood up at church meetings to denounce it.

My parents adopted many Asian values, especially a deep respect for the wisdom and experience of older people. I am grateful for the relationships I've had with older people who have encouraged me in special ways. Professor Wilcox was 97 when I met him, and he helped me to believe in myself in a way no one else was able to at that stage of my life. I still make a point of seeking out older people for friendship, advice and encouragement.

Mom and Dad were committed to their friends. Among their closest friends in the Tibetan work were Betty and Bob Ekvall and their son, David. The Ekvalls and my parents were drawn together by the tragedies they experienced in the field. My parents' third child was a boy named David Don. He died when he was six months old. My father made a simple wooden box, placed David's body in it, and then packed up the family for the two-day horseback ride to the Ekvalls' home, where they grieved together. Some time later, David Ekvall was killed in a freak accident. Later, Betty died of anthrax disease. Bob had ordered the newly discovered antibiotic that could cure anthrax, but it didn't reach their village in time to save her life.

Uncle Bob wandered away from the Lord for many years after experiencing these losses, yet I never heard a word of criticism from either of my parents aimed toward him. They continued to pray for him faithfully and reached out to him as a friend. A few years before he died, he returned to the Lord.

My mother came to live with us after we had returned from

Papua New Guinea. She was seventy-two, and she obviously enjoyed the chance to be with her son, daughter-in-law and grandchildren. She transmitted to our children qualities that can be modeled in no other way. She helped them to love the Word of God and encouraged them to memorize Scripture.

She was very affirming about what she experienced in our home. We talked about some of our differences; the way we were raising our kids was so different from how she had done it. One evening she said in a very reflective way, "If I had to do it over again, I'd do it differently." I was surprised, even taken aback, by this statement, and asked her what she meant. She explained that she had come to a different conclusion about what "seek first the Kingdom" meant for us as Christians. She could see that it was very God-honoring for us to include our children as part of our ministry. I'm sure there were some areas where she might still have disagreed with us, but it was very affirming for Shelby and me to hear her approval of our basic commitment to make a priority of our children as part of our ministry.

The resolution of those fierce conflicts of my adolescence, and the respect that my parents and I developed for one another were important signs for me of God's healing work in my life. I remember those stormy conflicts, but it is hard to remember the pain involved. I don't feel it any more. It's hard to even remember what it felt like. The many open wounds in my heart as a young man have been graciously healed by the Lord.

# 9

# *Healing through Marriage*

---

**M**any people in my life have contributed to the healing and growth that I have experienced, but no one has had a greater impact than Shelby. Over the course of more than twenty-five years of marriage, her love and encouragement have motivated my growth and helped me to have hope.

Shelby grew up in a dysfunctional family, too, although it was very different from my parents' home. Her parents married young and had five children in a short time. There wasn't much communication in their home. Shelby was never aware of conflict between her parents; her father just walked out when she was thirteen years old. This lack of communication made it extremely difficult for Shelby to express her feelings, especially in the context of conflict. It took me some time to discover the connection between my anger and criticism and Shelby's stomach aches. She would try to hold her hurt feelings in, but her body found a way to release the tension.

I am grateful for some positive aspects of Shelby's childhood; they have helped us in many ways. Shelby's mother was a strong Christian, and a wise woman in many ways. They never had much, but she helped them to feel that they were not poor. They always had something they could share with someone else in need. Even more importantly, she trusted her children. It was somewhat astonishing to me that she trusted them so much. After all, it made much more sense that someone who had been left with responsibility for five children with no resources or security would find it hard to trust anyone. But she trusted those kids, and they became trustworthy.

When Shelby and I married we decided to trust each other unconditionally. It was not a natural thing for me. In a sense, my parents had trusted me—perhaps too much for my own good. I had learned how to manipulate them. I always had some scheme ready to con my mother into giving me money. One of the few times my father actually caught me coming home drunk (a squeaky attic step woke him up), I made up a story about the drinks being spiked at a party. He wanted to know who was responsible, so he could prosecute them. Of course I couldn't give him a name because the whole story was a lie. Still, he didn't push too hard for the truth that night.

I knew I hadn't been trustworthy, and I was more or less programmed not to trust others. Nevertheless, Shelby and I decided that we had to trust one another and that it would be easier to trust if we had committed ourselves to trusting and being trustworthy. I don't ever remember our having a problem with jealousy, and as our kids came along, we learned to trust them in ways appropriate to their development.

Trust has become a fundamental principle in my life. It is the basis of any relationship, and if trust is abrogated, the relationship is in trouble. This was something we taught our kids. If we ever caught them lying, we stopped everything to deal with the issue. We wanted them to understand that trust is basic: we had to be able to trust them, and they had to be able to trust us.

When our eldest daughter, Paula, entered her senior year in high school, we decided to impute extraordinary trust to her. We felt that if she were not ready to make most of her own decisions during that year, she would not be ready to be on her own in college the next year.

We sat down with her and told her that she could come and go as she pleased. She didn't have to ask permission about how late she could stay out, who she would be with or what she would be doing. We only asked that she would do us the courtesy of telling us about her schedule ahead of time. I told her that I don't have to ask permission of Shelby, but I always try to let her know my plans.

Our plan worked superbly with Paula. In fact, she asked our advice more than she probably would have under the old system. But then there was Melody. Two people couldn't have more dissimilar personalities. As Melody approached her last year of high school, she seemed overly influenced by her peers. There were times when I repented of my foolishness in initiating this "trust business." I thought, "I'm going to change it. I'll never be able to follow through with Melody." We prayed a lot, and we went through with our plan to trust Melody. Despite our fears, she too proved trustworthy.

Another important contribution that came from Shelby's background and character was her decision to never criticize me, and to make our home a place of nurture and encouragement. I wasn't even aware of this commitment until twenty years into our marriage, but I certainly benefitted from it. Shelby had had a Bible teacher at Bryan College named Dr. Rader. Dr. Rader taught that the family should be the place where we felt affirmed and built up. Out in the world many people would say and do things to tear us down, but the family should be a place of refuge. Shelby took this advice seriously and made it a life principle never to criticize me, either directly to my face or to anyone else. She would always talk positively about me in front of the kids and would not tolerate criticism or disrespect from them either. Her commitment to affirm helped to build my fragile self-confidence and contributed to the process of healing the hurts and insecurities I brought into our marriage.

Nevertheless, despite these very positive commitments and our deep love for one another, our dysfunctional pasts created problems in some aspects of our marriage. I knew that it wasn't right that my father had never communicated his love to me, and I was determined to do things differently. I was starved for words and deeds that would tell me that I was loved, but for the first three years of our marriage the words "I love you" would not come out of my mouth. I wasn't used to hearing them. My parents had never said those words to me, nor even to each other in my hearing. I loved Shelby; I just didn't know how to say it.

This was not healthy for Shelby. She struggled for years with the fear that I would simply walk out, as her father had. My not being able to put my love for her into words, along with my bouts of destructive anger and criticism, left her wondering what kind of security she had in our relationship.

For a long time it was hard for me to pray with Shelby. In my parents' home, my mother had been the dominant spiritual leader in our family. She drilled Scripture verses into us, and she was determined that we would have a time of family worship each day. It was obvious to me that my father felt some pressure to go along with Mom's systematic approach to family devotions. We felt manipulated into it, and some of those feelings persisted when Shelby and I tried to find ways to pray together and build one another spiritually. We still don't pray together every day, but it has become something we both enjoy and appreciate.

Neither of us had a healthy model of how to resolve conflicts. My parents argued from time to time, but it was something they tried to hide. As kids we could tell something was going on—the tension was tangible—but we never saw how they resolved their differences. I know they argued about money: my father was extremely frugal, and my mother was always giving away everything she had.

When we lived in the same house as my parents during the first few years of our marriage, we fought fairly often. As soon as I came downstairs, my father would start into me. He didn't particularly care what we were arguing about, but he would exhort me to be more careful with the precious asset that Shelby was to me. That was good advice, but he didn't tell me how to do it better.

Gradually we have learned to resolve our differences in more constructive ways. I didn't want to repeat the model of hushed arguments behind closed doors that I had grown up with. We developed a pattern that was more honest. If an argument started in front of any other member of the family, we might go off by ourselves for a while to work it out, but we would always get the kids together later to let them know that we had reconciled. I would usually ask their forgiveness and ask Shelby's forgiveness in front of them. I wanted my kids to see the loop closed, to see that conflicts could be reconciled and resolved and that Shelby and I forgave each other.

We have tried to take seriously the biblical command to "not let the sun go down on your anger." We make every effort to resolve conflict promptly and deal with the hurts and anger. We discovered the importance of being very precise about what we're asking the other person to forgive. It's easy to say "I'm sorry," but it's much more significant to say "Shelby, will you forgive me for saying this hurtful word or for doing that specific action." It has a remarkable power to assuage the hurt feelings involved in the conflict. And when she reciprocates and says, "Yes, I forgive you," we have both participated in an act of the will to forgive, reconcile and put the anger behind us. God's principles are wonderfully healing and powerful in those situations.

These lessons have taken years and some painful experiences to learn. One of the hardest times for us was our last year in Papua New Guinea and our first year back in the States. I had been involved in discussions about decentralizing some of the operations and services that were provided in Ukarumpa, including education, in order to help reverse the trend of translators spending more time in Ukarumpa than in the villages. One of my friends challenged me: "You're tied to Ukarumpa with a ball and chain," he said. I had to admit I was comfortable there. I was full of talk about individualized education and other things I knew nothing about, so Shelby and I began to pray about how to put our convictions into action. We volunteered to go start a small elementary school in an outlying village where there was a training program for national translators. We were administrators, teachers and houseparents for the school in Wayembange that year.

We had quite a challenge before us. One of the girls in the school was a pathological liar. If you think of everything you hate in other people's children, she embodied all those qualities, and her parents were no help. She lived with us Monday through Friday, and by the end of the week she'd be behaving fairly well. Then she'd spend the weekend with her parents, and on Monday we were facing a little monster again. I didn't give up on the girl, but I did give up on her parents. That ongoing struggle, along with a series of other crises and conflicts, just wore us out.

The stress was affecting our relationship, and deep-seated issues were starting to come to the surface. Shelby had developed some resentments that she was having a hard time dealing with. She felt that I had opportunities to travel and do all kinds of exciting things, while she stayed home and changed diapers. I was away three or four months of the year, and she was playing Mom and Dad to four kids. More importantly, I wasn't helping her to feel like she was a partner with me, a vital part of everything I was did.

At some point we realized that something had to change. We thought that the problem was rooted in the fact that I was trying to do two jobs. That's when we decided to transfer back to the United States and focus on just one job. It soon became obvious that was an illusion. I hadn't dealt with my workaholism, and so I let one job absorb all my time and energy. At the same time Shelby's health was breaking down completely, although it took me a long time to realize it. Fortunately, about this time we began to get some professional help in dealing with the real issues.

One night we got into one of the worst fights we've ever had. It was a Saturday night, and we argued into the morning hours, with the argument becoming more rancorous and destructive as it went on. The next morning we went to church, probably more out of our sense of responsibility to get the kids to Sunday school than anything else. It was communion Sunday, and I felt there was no way I could take communion. So I sat in the pew struggling with my feelings, whispering to Shelby. Finally we went forward to receive communion.

It was the tradition in this church for each family to kneel together at one of the altar rails on either side of the platform. The pastor or one of the elders would pray for the family as they served communion. I remember the man who prayed for us that day—he was a lawyer we had gotten to know slightly. He had no idea what we were going through, just that we were missionaries on furlough. He prayed an absolutely God-inspired prayer, asking for healing in our relationship and for mending of things that went way back in our lives. It was just a few sentences, one of dozens of prayers he prayed that morning, but we both got up from the altar with tears just running down our faces.

When we got home I said to Shelby, "I think we need counseling." That was a very important thing for Shelby to hear. Up to that point she had believed that she was the source of our problems and thought I believed that too. By admitting that we needed help I made us equal partners in finding a solution to our problems. We joined a group for couples set up by Wycliffe's counseling office. It wasn't exactly the help we needed, but we started to find help in other areas after that.

Shelby attended some seminars and workshops that helped her to understand her unique gifts and to appreciate the contribution she could make to the things we were involved in, even though it was very different from mine. Shelby had tended to compare herself with others, especially me, in an absolute sense, as if there were only one right way to be. In the process of discovering her own gifts, she learned to resist that inclination and realized that there are differences in the way God made us; it's not a matter of right and wrong.

God gifted Shelby in the area of helping others, me in administration. When she was trying to imitate me, she would be torn between trying to be very organized and her desire to help others. At Ukarumpa, for example, she would do things like help another missionary woman clean up her house because she realized the woman was having trouble balancing all her responsibilities, but our house wouldn't get cleaned. Then she'd feel bad for not being organized enough to have been able to manage both tasks.

Several years later we both took the Meyers-Briggs Personality Profile and were surprised to learn that we are almost exactly alike, except in one area. Shelby's personality motivates her to keep options open; for her closure is not necessary. On the other hand I make decisions rather easily and like to see things resolved. This discovery added to the foundation of understanding her strengths and weaknesses and pursuing her gifts. Along the way, I've tried to encourage her development, though it's still a struggle for me to know how to offer the appropriate kind of encouragement.

For example, when Shelby wanted to fulfill her long-held goal to get a master's degree, I didn't feel I was wise in my encouragement. Since her health was very poor, she probably shouldn't have attempted a heavy academic program at that point. Again, it wasn't obvious that her educational goals fit in with our future plans, since we were no longer teaching missionary kids, and I was moving into a more administrative role. But it was important to her, and I supported her in it.

She wasn't able to finish that program before we moved to Dallas, but several years ago, when we had moved back to California, she decided to pursue an M.A. in Human Resources Development at Azusa Pacific University. Looking back I'm not sure that my way of encouraging her has always been helpful. Sometimes it felt like I was putting pressure on her. Shelby is always a busy person, and it wasn't easy for her to finish the program. Now that she's finished, she says she's grateful I pushed her a bit because it was an important milestone for her, but at the time I felt more like a parent who wants to protect a child from the consequences of her behavior than a partner encouraging her to reach for her goal.

Our marriage has been a lifelong experiment in learning how to love one another. It's a challenge for me to discover how to do what's really best for Shelby, not just what I think is best. Trust and commitment are the foundations of the growth in our relationship. If we hadn't decided to be committed and trust one another, much of the healing and growth that we have experienced as individuals and as a couple could never have happened.

# 10

# Breaking
# the Cycle

*D*ad, did you pray for us a lot when we were kids?"
Melody asked one day. I didn't know how to respond.
Why was she asking? But we had indeed prayed a lot
for our children, so I said, "Yes, of course we did. But
why do you ask?"

Melody explained that she had been thinking about a family
that had just spent the weekend with us. They are good friends
from our college days, but their family dynamics were very
different from ours. Our friends are good Christians and have
tried to be good parents, but their children seemed so
troubled. In contrast to my daughters, my friend's kids re-

minded me of my youth.

The legacy of dysfunctional families is crippled children who become crippled adults. As often as not they in turn raise their own crippled children, passing on the hurts of their past to the next generation. How can the cycle be broken?

The process of being reconciled with my own father gave me hope that things could be different for my children, but as in so many areas of my life, learning to be a good parent was harder than I thought it would be. As I reflected on my relationship with my parents I determined that I would communicate love and respect to my children, befriend them and believe in them. Learning to make this a reality has been a matter of trial and error—and much prayer.

I still remember the shock I felt when a friend of mine told me he would be glad when his first child was at least five or six because then the child would have a personality. *What was he talking about?* I wondered. I could see the personality in Paula within her first few days at home. I talked to her, and to each of her sisters, long before they could talk back.

In our family, communication has become one of the foundational points of our relationships. Shelby and I have learned to make the effort to listen to our kids and to share information and concerns with them as well. Family meals are a key to our communication. Our evening meals have become a time for us to catch up with one another's activities and experiences, to share ideas and to affirm one another. We tried to resist the tendency to use those times for solving problems or for correcting or disciplining one of the kids.

We have also made it a principle not to face one another with yesterday's sins or offenses. As a child, I was constantly reminded of my past failings. Instead of motivating me to do better, as I'm sure my parents intended, they became expectations for future failures. I never experienced the grace of having my offense forgiven and forgotten as a child. This is part of our commitment to not let the sun go down on our anger—we attempt to deal with problems promptly and put them behind us.

In my experience, discipline had equaled humiliation. My parents had been taught that it was their responsibility to break the will of their children—that was their interpretation of "spare the rod, spoil the child." Some of us had stronger wills than others, and we got more discipline. My brother Frank probably got more than any of us. At different periods my Dad did a lot of traveling and speaking in churches. He was the enforcer of discipline in our home, so when he got home, our transgressions were reported to him, and we would be punished. Frank always knew he was going to get a spanking, so he figured he might as well earn it. In this battle of wills we felt we were winning by smoking and drinking; Dad tried to win by over-disciplining us.

I knew I had to discipline my kids. Scripture says it is the parents' responsibility to train the children to follow the Lord: "Fathers, do not exasperate your children; instead, bring them up in the training and instruction of the Lord" (Eph 6:4). I wanted them to know that I respected them and loved them, even when they had disobeyed and needed discipline.

A number of years ago, one of the girls was caught pilfering money she had collected for a school fund-raising project. I was on a trip when this was discovered, and a very angry and hurt Shelby picked me up at the airport. She filled me in on the problem. I felt embarrassed, hurt and angry, and terribly disappointed that one of my daughters would do such a thing.

*117*

By the time we got home, our daughter had thought it all through. She acknowledged her guilt and responsibility. She expressed genuine regret for her actions, not just for getting caught. She had come up with a course of discipline that was much more severe than the plan we had discussed on the way home. By the end of our conversation, I actually felt a measure of pride in her willingness to own up to her misdeed and face the consequences.

I hadn't respected my Dad growing up, and I didn't think he respected me. In contrast, Shelby and I have tried to let the girls know that we believe in them. By God's grace, the message has gotten through. As the girls have grown up and gotten to know peers from very different backgrounds, they have let us know that our efforts to communicate our love and respect for them were successful. Once when Paula was a freshman at Wheaton College, I was traveling through Chicago and stopped by to see her. As we talked over dinner, she told me, "Daddy, you're a real friend. You're the kind of adult I would choose for a friend." No one could have paid me a higher compliment!

As a missionary kid myself, I wanted my children to appreciate the unique opportunities that our lifestyle offered them, not to be embarrassed by it as I was by my parents' ministry. Melody wrote us from college that a friend had remarked that she was "different" in a way that we must be proud of. "The more I thought about what he said," she wrote, "the more I began to realize that you two have given me a beautiful gift. You believe in me! And I have come to believe in myself. It has made me different."

During the year Paula was teaching in China, I had the opportunity to travel there to help locate a site for a summer project for InterVarsity. Paula arranged to take some time off and meet me in Beijing.

It was delightful to meet my very adult daughter in the country where I was born and where my parents had pioneered for nearly twenty-five years. I was impressed by how well she had adjusted. She got us on the right trains, bought tickets, arranged meals, found the rest rooms, handling all the details involved in traveling in a foreign country with ease.

One day she took me into a tiny little restaurant for some special dumplings. As we were waiting for our food, various people passed by and acknowledged us. Paula greeted them in proper Chinese. Then she struck up a conversation with an old man who was allowing his dinner to settle. They talked for twenty-five minutes of animated conversation, laughing and obviously enjoying one another's company. I knew Paula had not studied Chinese; she had spent most of the past eight months teaching English to high-school teachers, but she had picked up quite a bit of conversational Chinese. After the man said goodbye and left, I told Paula how impressed I was. "Oh Daddy, it's nothing," she replied. "They all ask the same questions."

In Qiqihar, where Paula had been teaching, I saw how well respected she was by everyone there. The president of the university told me she had won an award as the best young teacher. In her classroom it was apparent that her students not only respected her, they loved her. My respect and appreciation of her rose even higher on my two-day train ride back to Beijing. I hadn't realized how much she had done for me until I had to take care of those details on my own.

That China experience was valuable encouragement, because it wasn't always easy to make our kids believe that they are special and that being different in some ways is OK. When we moved back to the United States after nine years in Papua New Guinea, Melody had just finished second grade, but it was the middle of the school year in California. She could repeat part of second grade or jump ahead into the second half of third grade. We decided to put her in third grade, and although she fell behind a bit academically and socially, she was managing. The thing that really bothered her was her height. She was the shortest in her class. Nothing that Shelby and I could say made her feel good about herself. Her shortness undermined her self-esteem.

Summer vacation came as a relief; playing with kids of various ages, her height didn't seem to be such a problem. Shelby was surprised and delighted when Melody came bounding through the door after her first day in fourth grade. "Mother, mother, mother! Guess what!" she exclaimed. "You'll never believe this. I, Melody Harrison, am the tallest of the short kids in my class!" She had finally found something she could feel good about in being short.

Shelby and I always believed that our responsibility to our children was an integral part of our ministry for God, not something in competition with serving God. We have attempted in all kinds of ways to include them in our ministry, without exploiting them. I remember my resentment at being dragged from town to town in New York, as my parents pioneered Sunday schools and reopened churches. They would often hold six to eight meetings a week, and I had to attend every meeting that did not interfere with school. I was supposed to be an example, praying or sharing a testimony on cue. Anytime I misbehaved, which I did regularly, I would be brought up short and severely punished.

I didn't want my kids to feel forced to perform or participate.

When we lived in Ukarumpa, Shelby decided that she would rather not hire servants to help her run the household, which is a common practice, given the lack of conveniences most Westerners are accustomed to. Our concern was partly not to let our standard of living separate us from the people around us, and partly to help the girls learn to be responsible. We had people in our home frequently, and the girls were always part of our hospitality, through serving as well as participating in the conversation.

Shortly before we returned to America, Papua New Guinea received its independence from Australia. A number of Wycliffe representatives, including Shelby and me, were invited to meet the first prime minister of the country. Holly was a baby, and we took her with us. There was a rather awkward moment during that meeting when Shelby realized she needed to change Holly's diaper. Much to our amazement the new prime minister guided them to a table nearby, and Holly had her diaper changed in the prime minister's office.

The girls were used to helping out around the house, and we naturally extended that participation to tasks that needed to be done for our ministry. They stuffed envelopes, ran mimeograph and copy machines. At age ten, Holly served as my receptionist for a summer. I didn't know whether she could handle the job, but we decided to give it a try. She was remarkably effective in that role. When we were serving with English Language Institute/China, the organization was growing so rapidly we could barely keep up with the exploding number of teachers being sent to China. Our first summer all four of them pitched in to help us put together training materials, process donations and provide hospitality. We couldn't have done it without their help.

Currently, both Paula and Melody, as well as Shelby, are working with me in the Mission Division of InterVarsity. Sometimes it's too much of a good thing. Shelby and I especially have to discipline ourselves not to talk about work twenty-four hours a day. We both love what we do, but we recognize that we'll end up resenting and hating it if that's all we talk about. She has made some conscious efforts to get involved in other activities, from finishing her M.A. to joining women's groups, in order to bring some balance into our lives. Our daughters have less tolerance for constant discussions of work, so they help us too.

We try to keep the girls informed about what is happening with us. We ask for their input on decisions, especially ones that affect them. Each time we've moved and whenever I've been considering a new ministry opportunity, we've consulted them. Their input has been very mature. We've talked about how a change would affect them—moving to a new city, new schools, new relationships and leaving friends behind.

My ministry has almost always involved travel, and sometimes a third of the year or more I would be away from home. I wanted the girls to know what I was doing, where I was going, when I'd be back. Very often I would take one of them with me on a trip. Whether they see it firsthand or hear my report afterward, I want them to have a sense of fulfillment and accomplishment in what God is doing around the world.

How does a child develop a sense of who they are? Much of it comes from their sense of who their parents are—what people think of them, what our colleagues, people from church or the community think of them. Those things contribute to their sense of identity. By traveling with me or hearing stories from my trips, they can get a sense of who I am in other people's eyes.

Last year Holly traveled with Shelby and me to the Soviet Union as we set up an exchange program for Soviet and American students. Recently, I was at a board meeting where one of the students who participated in that program shared her experience from the summer and read a letter from her Soviet counterpart. It was very important for me to tell Holly and the other girls about that, because they know how close to my heart that program is, and in a sense, they have a stake in it too.

Along the way many of my convictions about children never being separated from their parents for the sake of ministry have mellowed. I've seen a trend in some contemporary teaching on the family that borders on idolatry. Some people hold that it is absolutely immoral for children to be separated from their families. Sometimes it's a rationalization for homeschooling, the idea that parents must be in total control of the input the child receives. Some missions agencies have seen a decline in the number of young families who are willing to serve because they are unwilling to tolerate any kind of separation from their children. Limiting missionaries to childless couples and single people could seriously hamper the world mission of the church. I was not too far from that position for a number of years. I felt that God meant for kids to be with parents, and God would bless any mission that made a priority of helping kids to stay with their parents. I certainly tried to build that into the programs we ran in Papua New Guinea.

However, Shelby and I have come to the conclusion that the issue is not simply the quantity of time together, but the quality of the relationship. She felt strongly that my relationship with our girls was better by far than the relationships in lots of families who are always together physically, but where the child never has the total attention of the parents. I made it a point to set aside time when the girls would have my full attention. For a number of years I had one evening a week set aside, and each week I would have a "date" with one of my daughters. They chose the activity, and we would play together. After a while, I learned to design the activity to facilitate conversation, so we could catch up and care for one another in ways that we couldn't do when I was traveling.

Along the way, I've gotten to know kids who were separated from their families by circumstances or policy for periods of time, yet they always knew they were high priorities for their parents. They carried on correspondence that was very loving and affirming. The kids didn't doubt their parents' love or concern; they knew they were important. Ministry doesn't have to conflict with healthy family life; finding the right balance takes effort and creativity, but the rewards are well worth it.

Perhaps the most rewarding thing for me to see in my children is their ability to contribute to our family their own brand of encouragement and affirmation. The ideal of the family being a place where we find refuge and are built up in love is happening, not only because Shelby and I make an effort to live this way, but because our children do too.

I still remember one Friday night I came home from the office weary and discouraged. It had been a brutal week, with some of the most difficult problems I had ever faced in my role as vice president for development for Wycliffe flooding in on me. I was feeling all of my old insecurities, and I knew I wasn't responding well to the challenges. I walked into the kitchen, and Holly, who was ten at the time, was standing on the opposite side of the room. She took a long look at me, and then just bolted across the kitchen. She hugged me and looked into my eyes and said, "I love you, Daddy." It undid me. All the discouragement and difficulties of the past week drained away. Immediately I felt better.

My girls saved Father's Day a couple of years ago, when Shelby and I got into a terrible argument. It was Sunday morning, and against my will and my better judgment, we went to church. The argument continued, even as we walked into church. During the service I was reflecting on my wounds when the pastor called on me to give a testimony about how I had experienced God's grace that week. I barely heard my name, and quickly turned to Melody to find out what I had been asked. I stood up and acknowledged I hadn't been listening, thinking of a response while people laughed.

At home the argument continued. We had planned a special celebration for Father's Day and had invited Phil Evans, a local InterVarsity campus worker, to join us. It was taking us a long time to get to the bottom of our discussion, so the girls fixed dinner. Phil arrived and wondered where we were. "Just listen and you'll know," one of them answered. He could hear our raised voices from the bedroom.

When they told us the meal was on the table, it took me a few minutes to decide that I should join the family. Sullen and angry, I sat silently at the end of the table. The girls were determined to communicate their love to me and affirm me on that Father's Day. At the end of the meal, one by one they began to tell me about the things they appreciated and loved in me. They hadn't gotten very far when I began to feel the tension leave me. My anger was gone, and I could see that I had to apologize to Shelby. Since the girls and Phil were so aware of our argument, I asked her to forgive me right there.

The entire family left the table that day relieved and buoyed up through affirmation and encouragement.

Another time Tonya was going through a hard time in her life. One of her sisters decided to give her a reminder of our affirmations of her. She wrote and drew a beautiful page of "Tonya, we appreciate you because . . ." A year or two later one of Tonya's friends was looking at her photo album and discovered this page. "What in the world is this?" she wanted to know. After Tonya's explanation a tearful friend responded, "Wow, your family really loves you, don't they?"

Our kids know we love them in a way I never knew my parents loved me. The cycle has been broken—or at least largely disabled. I still see some remnants of my problems with anger in one or two of my girls, but I don't see the massive insecurities and wounds that I entered adulthood with.

The impact our family dynamics have on other people is surprising and rewarding to us as well. A number of years ago I was in Singapore, helping to open an office there for Wycliffe. I met a young man named Brian Leong, who told me of his plans to come to the United States to prepare for ministry. I invited him to stay in our home.

After spending a few days with us, Brian told us that he was an orphan. He became our "adopted" son, even though he was over eighteen when we met him. He lived with us for several years, and he is genuinely part of our family. He told us once that he considered the years he spent with us "a living seminar on family education."

When Paula was preparing to go to China, I had the opportunity to lead devotions during the training program. Another young woman in the group was struck by the interaction she observed between Paula and me. She wrote me a long letter telling how she had been encouraged by our love for each other. It was a dramatic contrast, she explained, to the painful relationship she had had with her father, who had died a short while previously. Later she wrote this song:

### A Father's Love

When I saw you with your daughter
   I knew that God was near,
'Cause I felt my heart fill with joy
   and my eyes were filled with tears.

The love I felt between you two I cannot quite describe,
   for it was a love not known to me, ever in my life.
Through the love I have seen that you have shared
   our God reaches out to me,
Saying, "This is how I love you, child,
   the precious child I see.
The love I want for you to know comes not from human
     souls,
   but only from above, my child, I have planted and it
     grows."

So I listened to my heavenly Father
   as I watched your daughter glow,
and God then showed me something else I needed now to
     know.
He said, "Child of mine,
   your earthly father loved you more than you can know,
   but I let you feel the pain so long
   so closer to me you'd grow.

I love you so that it breaks my heart
  when it's hard for you to see me there
  so I brought you this man and his precious girl
  to show you how much I care."

It's a cliché to say that children are our hope for the future, but when I look at our daughters and see individuals who are so much more healthy and balanced than I remember myself being at their ages, my hope is renewed. God's faithfulness to Shelby and me in helping us raise children who are not scarred as we were is simply staggering. Can the dysfunctional family cycle be broken? I have four wonderful reasons to say it can be.

# 11

## *In Weakness Made Strong*

*D*uring our early years in Papua New Guinea we met a missionary family while we were vacationing at the coast. My heart went out to their two boys, who were about sixteen and eighteen. Their parents, much like my parents, were having difficulty balancing the demands of ministry and the needs of their kids. The mother had been supervising their education through correspondence courses, but both boys had gotten stuck in the middle of ninth grade and hadn't made any progress for years. Meanwhile they were very active in their parent's ministry, doing all the things their parents were doing. They had some real advantages—they could speak in front of groups, think on their feet and make good decisions. But they couldn't write a simple English sentence. I persuaded the parents to let us take the boys back to Ukarumpa and try to get them through ninth grade, at least.

I remember looking at some of their early chicken scratchings and wondering if they would ever learn to write. They were wondering the same thing too. I invested a lot of hours with them trying to reassure them that they could learn. They didn't believe they could do it.

The school itself was a difficult environment for them. Mission schools tend to be homogenous and, unfortunately, not very tolerant of differences. These boys were quite a bit older than their classmates, which was embarrassing for them. They had to eat a lot of crow, but they made it. One of them later went on to become a missionary pilot and returned to Papua New Guinea.

Looking back, in some sense I am amazed at the trust their parents placed in me. I was no great expert in education and certainly hadn't been trained to offer remedial help to two kids who had been out of school for years. I was only a few years older than they were, yet I sensed that what they needed was an opportunity and some encouragement. In many ways their situation was like mine when I was their age—I hadn't spent much time in school and didn't think I had the ability to learn either.

Throughout my life there have been many experiences like this one where God took a weakness from my past and through it enabled me to help someone else. That very process has contributed greatly to my growth and recovery, showing me again and again that God's love and good intentions for me transcend the hurts of the past.

A short time after we moved to Dallas in the mid-seventies, we began to hear distressing news about our friends the Staalsens in Papua New Guinea. They were considering taking a leave of absence from missionary work.

Phil had been an important person in our lives. When we had arrived at Ukarumpa as new missionaries, I was a bit disappointed at the lack of intellectual stimulation there. We had come to the field straight from graduate school and had been involved in a small group who were dedicated to challenging assumptions and pushing each other to the limits of our understanding. Everyone was telling me I should meet Phil Staalsen. I heard that so much I was almost determined not to like the guy, but when we did finally meet it was clear from the start we were kindred spirits. Phil was tremendously gifted; he had an amazing ability to understand complex truth, whether linguistic theory or theology, and articulate it simply and clearly.

By our last year in Papua New Guinea, when we were living out in Wayembange, Phil and Lori had finished one New Testament translation and had moved to Wayembange to pioneer a program to train Papua New Guineans to be Bible translators. The four of us spent a lot of time together that year and were very close friends. So we were naturally concerned when we began to hear that the Staalsens were returning to the United States.

They visited us in Dallas on their way home to Chicago. I had no plan in mind except somehow to encourage Phil to continue in mission work but, in the course of the time we spent together at our home, I had a very strong intuition that I should invite him to come work for me. I've learned to trust those intuitions.

Phil thought the idea was improbable. He didn't wholly approve of the personnel buildup in the international and division home office.

They continued on their way to Chicago, but not long afterward we got a phone call. Phil had been praying about my offer.

Phil arrived, and although he was a very intelligent and talented person, he didn't feel secure about the position. I was heading the development division, but his background was in anthropology and linguistics. I tried to encourage him that he had qualities that would be beneficial. I tried to provide for him what I try to provide for anybody who works with me—a climate in which one is secure and is able to grow.

Phil soon began to enjoy himself and grow into the position. He had committed himself to serve about two years, and when that time was up I tried to encourage him to stay longer, but he was headed toward graduate school.

About that time my boss was looking for a vice president of finance. It wasn't the first thought that came to mind, but one day I mentioned Phil as a candidate. My boss didn't see the connection at first. Phil had little background in accounting or finance. But as we talked more about it, he began to see that Phil's leadership and relational skills would be a real advantage, and he was smart enough to know that he would have to rely on specialists in the areas where he didn't have the training or experience. We worked together for several years on the vice-presidential team after that.

After so many people believed in me when I thought I was worthless, it isn't hard for me to believe in others. I've always been an optimist, and it's an attitude I cultivate deliberately. I choose to see the glass as half-full, not half-empty. I see the potential in people and situations, and that makes the risks worth taking. The opportunities I have had to serve as an administrator and leader in various mission organizations have given me the chance to put into practice the principles God has taught me in the course of my recovery.

Seeing God develop in my family a lifestyle of love and affirmation, and watching him turn my areas of weakness into strengths in ministry have been the greatest joys in my life. They are the evidence of God's healing and redeeming work in me. I am privileged to be able to share them with my coworkers and others.

Many of the principles that guide my leadership or management style at the office are the same ones Shelby and I have learned to put into practice in our family life: love, trust, respect, servanthood. Studies suggest that what motivates people is not money but vision and the provision of affirmation and encouragement. People are motivated when they feel that a leader believes in them and cares about them personally.

The idea of servant leadership has become popular in the business world these days, but it's as old and as important as Jesus washing his disciples' feet. I still remember George Cowan, then the president of Wycliffe, being the first to volunteer for dishes or some other menial task at the Summer Institute of Linguistics we attended when we joined Wycliffe. I found it somewhat shocking to see the president of the mission doing dishes, but it demonstrated that he didn't think himself too good to do whatever needed to be done just because he was at the top of the organizational chart.

I've found it's important to be willing to do anything I ask a subordinate to do and to be flexible enough to reach out and meet their needs. As a leader in a Christian organization, I have a pastoral responsibility to those I work with. Sometimes I become aware of a problem floating under the surface—someone seems unusually tense or frustrated or two people seem to be having a hard time getting along. I make it a point to try to help the people involved to resolve their conflict.

I also try to take my managers on a retreat periodically and to focus that time on building one another up. There are always plenty of work-related issues to talk about, but we deliberately structure our agenda so that we focus on getting to know one another better and affirming each other. I ask questions designed to let them give a snapshot of their background, and we talk about how each person is doing now. We talk about things we are thankful for, evidence of God's blessing in our ministry over the past several months. We share concerns and pray for one another.

A very special portion of our retreats is the time we focus on each person individually and affirm them. I encourage the others in the group to look the person we are affirming directly in the eye, and say, "One thing I appreciate about you is . . ." We have a big pad of paper and fill up an entire sheet with our affirmations of each person.

A few days after our last retreat, I wandered into the office of someone I consider one of the stronger managers on my team. She had her sheet of affirmations pinned to the wall. "I was having a bad day," she explained to me, "and I put that up there to remind me of the good things other people perceive in me."

As challenging and exciting as I find my role as a leader in a Christian ministry, there are times I struggle with the responsibilities and with my old weaknesses. One day I was feeling discouraged. I was struggling with anger but couldn't seem to get to the bottom of it. I had been in a series of meetings that had produced so much stress that just days before that I thought I was having a heart attack. My doctor diagnosed an ulcer. Someone knocked on my door, and I was happy to see it was a coworker whom I have talked to before when I needed some encouragement. Much to my chagrin, he began to dump his frustrations on me. "Good grief," I thought. "I'm not up to this today." I wasn't feeling strong enough to lift someone else up, but I breathed a prayer for wisdom as my friend shared his feelings. I listened and tried to give some encouragement and advice.

The next morning I was trying to have devotions when I had a very strong impression that I should follow the advice I had given my friend. What I had told him was to get the junk out, write down whatever was bothering him and ask himself if there was anything he could or should do to deal with it. I hadn't been able to put a label on what was bothering me; it was just a vague resentful feeling.

I followed my own advice, and pretty soon I had a list of twelve or fifteen things I was feeling resentful about. Some of them were irritations that had turned into resentments; they were trivial and I just decided then and there to forgive the persons involved and put the resentments aside. Others were more complex, and that morning I began to make appointments to talk with the people involved. One of them involved a member of my staff who had offended a business friend of mine. When I talked with her about it, I found out that she realized she had offended him and had already written to him to apologize. I was aware of the offense, but not the resolution, and it was still gnawing at me. In the process of getting these resentments out in the open and resolving the issues involved, all of my stress symptoms disappeared.

I am beginning to realize that much of my anger is triggered by fear as well as resentments. If I'm too busy and not spending enough time with the Lord, little resentments tend to build up and I don't deal with them well. It has also been important to face the fears that underlie my anger.

For a long time I thought that what I was most afraid of was the financial pressure of my job—what would happen if our division didn't raise enough money to cover its expenses. As I probed that fear and tried to be completely honest with myself, I had to admit that what I was really afraid of was failing, embarrassing myself or being compared with my predecessor. I didn't want others to think I had failed in the things they had entrusted to me.

It was embarrassing to acknowledge these fears and even more embarrassing to talk to my peers about them. Our culture doesn't encourage us to talk about our weaknesses; it trains us to cover them up. But I have discovered a surprising benefit of acknowledging my fears: in the light of day, those fears are exposed as lies. I don't have to live with the fear of failure hanging over me, because my life doesn't represent failure; it represents accomplishment and blessing. The Lord may allow me to fail in the task of keeping our accounts in the black for a particular fiscal year, but even that would not make me a failure as a person. The people around me are not expecting me to fail or comparing me with anyone else. The thing I'm most afraid of is a lie; what comforts me is the truth.

When Shelby and I were living in Papua New Guinea our friends the Franklins had the Living Bible paraphrase of Galatians 6:4 on a plaque in their home: "Let everyone be sure that he is doing his very best, for then he will have the personal satisfaction of work well done, and won't need to compare himself with someone else." We realized that we were often too concerned about what others thought of us and fell into the trap of comparing ourselves with others. The truth of this verse gripped our hearts. We memorized it, and it became a theme for our home and for the school in Ukarumpa. It has become something of a life verse for me, one that I still need to remind myself of from time to time. I remember as a child seeing the dynamics in some of my friends' homes and wishing that my family could be more "normal." My road might have been easier, but I don't regret the journey I've been on at all. The very things that caused me the most pain have been transformed by God into a source of growth for me and blessing to others. I'm grateful that God chooses to demonstrate his strength through my weakness.

# 12

# *The History of God's Faithfulness*

*O*ur family has a rather unique New Year's Day tradition. Instead of focusing on our resolutions for the coming year, we spend some time looking back at the year behind us.

We get out our Chinese firepot—a special pot shaped like a donut with a chimney in the middle. Charcoal briquettes go in the chimney, and a wonderful soup fills the pot. Then we sit around the table, and each person cooks their meat and vegetables, a little bit at a time, in the soup. The firepot is small, and on New Year's we generally have our whole family plus some friends, so the meal takes two or three hours.

The Chinese tradition is to tell stories during the meal. Usually the host starts by telling one story and then the others chime in with theirs. While each person tells a story, the others are cooking and eating their food. In our family, our stories recount the record of God's faithfulness to us during the previous year. Everyone, including our guests, is expected to have something to share.

Scripture says that God somehow inhabits our praise. We always feel the presence of the Holy Spirit in our midst on those days. We have fun, too, and laugh and joke with each other. But we take seriously the task of remembering and celebrating God's faithfulness to us.

Those times we set aside to remember how God has blessed us and helped us as a family during the year are crucial. Those stories are the things we have to rest on when doubts come or difficulties arise. When Paula was in China, she experienced a particularly difficult time in her own spiritual life. At one point she shared with her supervisor, "I'm not worried about the current state of my spiritual life. The history of God in my family is so strong that I know God is faithful."

I believe one of the strengths of our family lies not in the fact that we are perfect people or a perfect family—we certainly aren't—but in the way that our memory and traditions help us to deal with the difficult challenges we face in life. We support one another in crisis, and we know, individually and as a family, that we stand on the bedrock of God's love for us.

At one point not too many years ago, I suffered a major setback. I was in a working relationship in which I was trying hard to faithfully apply the things God had taught me, but it didn't look like we would be able to resolve our differences. I felt a total failure. I was as low as I'd ever been in my life.

In fact, I was so depressed that I didn't even trust myself to drive across town to a doctor's appointment. So Shelby drove me. As soon as we got in the car she said, "Pull out a piece of paper. I want you to write down something you like about yourself."

I couldn't come up with anything. I couldn't think of any realm of my life where I felt useful or had done something worthwhile. So Shelby started to come up with some things and told me to write them down: "I am an excellent husband. I am a child of the King. I am a great lover." At first I didn't believe those things. Then she had me read the list out loud. I felt like she was my mother telling me to eat my peas, but it was what I needed. By the time we reached the doctor's office I was feeling almost human again.

In our family we call this remembering the "givens"—those truths of our faith and of our experience of one another that form the basis of our hope. They are statements we accept without question: God loves us; we love each other. Some days the givens are hard to swallow, but even on the darkest days they are powerful. They remind me of how far God has brought me and my family toward wholeness. They remind me that I am not bound by my past; in Christ I have hope for a future where my healing will be complete.

# Resources for Recovery

**Secular books on dysfunctional families and codependence:**

Beattie, Melody. *Codependent No More*. San Francisco: Harper & Row, 1987. Focuses on those in relationship to alcoholics but offers a popular introduction to codependents of all types.

_____ . *Beyond Codependency and Getting Better All the Time*. San Francisco: Harper & Row, 1989. A sequel that looks at the recovery process.

Mellody, Pia, with Andrea Wells Miller and J. Keith Miller. *Facing Codependence*. San Francisco: Harper & Row, 1989. A look at codependence from the perspective of abused or deprived children.

Schaef, Anne Wilson. *Co-Dependence: Misunderstood—Mistreated*. San Francisco: Harper & Row, 1986. An attempt to synthesize various approaches to codependence under the umbrella of the "addictive process" of our culture.

*The Twelve Steps and Twelve Traditions*. New York: Alcoholics Anonymous World Service. The classic resource book on the Twelve Steps recovery process.

Whitfield, Charles L. *Healing the Child Within*. Deerfield Beach, Fla.: Health Communications, 1987. A psychological perspective on the recovery process for children of dysfunctional families.

**Christian books on issues related to dysfunction and codependence:**

Carlson, Dwight. *Overcoming Hurts and Anger*. Eugene, Ore.: Harvest House, 1981. A guide to handling anger and other negative emotions.

Mayers, Marvin K. *Christianity Confronts Culture*. Grand Rapids, Mich.: Zondervan, 1987. Offers a trust model of ministry based on acceptance of self and others.

Seamands, David A. *Healing for Damaged Emotions.* Wheaton, Ill.: Victor Books, 1981.

_____ *Putting Away Childish Things.* Wheaton, Ill.: Victor Books, 1984. Healing of memories as a step toward freedom and maturity.

Thompson, Bruce, and Barbara Thompson: *Walls of My Heart.* Euclid, Minn.: Crown Ministries International, 1989. A look at emotional pain and biblical principles for restoration.

*The Twelve Steps—A Spiritual Journey.* San Diego: Recovery Publications, 1988. A workbook through the Twelve Steps with Scripture references, including a guide for groups.

## Twelve Steps Groups

*There are Twelve Steps groups that are geared for specific types of addictive/compulsive behavior. The following organizations can put you in touch with local chapters in your area:*

Adult Children of Alcoholics
Central Service Board
P.O. Box 3216
Torrance, CA 90505
(213) 534-1815

Al-Anon/Alateen
Family Group Headquarters
Madison Square Station
New York, NY 10010
(212) 683-1771

Alcoholics Anonymous World
Services, Inc.
468 Park Avenue South
New York, NY 10016
(212) 686-1100

Co-Dependents Anonymous
P.O. Box 33577
Phoenix, AZ 85067-3577
(602) 944-0141

Debtors Anonymous
P.O. Box 20322
New York, NY 10025

Emotions Anonymous
P.O. Box 4245
St. Paul, MN 55104

Gamblers Anonymous
P.O. Box 17173
Los Angeles, CA 90017

Narcotics Anonymous
World Service Office
16155 Wyandotte Street
Van Nuys, CA 91406
(818) 780-3951

National Association for
Children of Alcoholics
31706 Coast Highway, Suite 201
South Laguna, CA 92677
(714) 499-3889

Overeaters Anonymous
World Service Office
2190 190th Street
Torrance, CA 90504
(213) 320-7941

Sexaholics Anonymous
P.O. Box 300
Simi Valley, CA 93062

## Christian Therapy Groups

Alcoholics for Christ
1316 N. Campbell Road
Royal Oak, MI 48067
(800) 441-7877

Alcoholics Victorious
National Headquarters
9370 S.W. Greenburg Road
Suite 411
Tigard, OR 97323
(503) 245-9629

Changing Lives Ministries
8196 Grapewin
P.O. Box 2325
Corona, CA 91718
(714) 734-4300

Christian Alcoholics
Rehabilitation Association
FOA Road
Pocahontas, MS 39072

Liontamers
2801 North Brea Blvd.
Fullerton, CA 92635
714) 529-5544

New Hope
FEFC Fullerton
2801 North Brea Blvd.
Fullerton, CA 92635
(714) 529-5544

New Life Treatment Center
P.O. Box 38
Woodstock, MN 56186

Overcomers Outreach
2290 West Whittier Blvd.
La Habra, CA 90631
(213) 697-3994

Substance Abusers Victorious
1 Cascade Plaza
Akron, OH 44308